Sinfully Healthy

Over 100 quick and easy recipes
for healthy living that taste great!

By Debbi Throckmorton Stinnett

Sinfully Healthy

Over 100 quick and easy recipes
for healthy living that taste great!

First Printing January 2002
2,000 copies
Second Printing July 2003
3,500 copies

ISBN: 0-9709787-0-7
Library of Congress Card Catalog #: 2001092706

Designed and Manufactured in the
United States of America by
Cookbook Resources
541 Doubletree Drive
Highland Village, Texas 75077
972/317-0245 • 972/317-6404 fax
Toll free: 866/229-2665
www.cookbookresources.com

Dedication

This book is in memory of my parents, John and Jane Throckmorton who gave me the confidence and courage to believe in myself, and to know that I could accomplish anything I set out to do. I will love them forever because of that.

Acknowledgment

After spending an endless amount of time creating this book, I know I could never have finished this without the help of so many people. I want to thank each and every one of them. Without their encouragement and their constant support, I would not have been able to finish this. I thank most of all my family, Matt, Blake and Steve - thank you all for being so patient with me, trying all of my recipes, and encouraging me to finish my book. I love you for that. I would like to give a special thanks to my husband Steve who helped me so much. He not only helped to create many of the recipes, but he was also my best critic and partner. Also, thanks to all of my family and friends who submitted some of their favorite recipes to me for the book. Without all of their recipes, I couldn't have put together this type of book. Also, Roxanne Mason who spent many hours analyzing all of my recipes. We corresponded in between our busy schedules to get this finished, and I thank her for her expertise and devotion.

These are all the family and friends that gave me their recipes to use in the book. I thank them from the bottom of my heart! Also, thanks all of you that have been behind me encouraging me to finish this book. I hope that as you read the book, you will have fun cooking and creating healthy meals that your family and friends will enjoy! Bon Appetit!

Kim Russell	Jeanette Hutcheson	Gretchen Heinz	Doris Stinnett
Eileen Stahlhut	Sandy Webster	Sue Throckmorton	Helen Behymer
Claudia Cole	Suzy Hamelink	Jill Seagrave	Melissa Hamelink

I also want to thank my two editors who spent their summer deciphering my written recipes and the analysis onto the computer disc for me. Meghan Stack and Erin Bellanti spent many hours in between their jobs and busy college social lives working on my recipes. I thank both of them from the bottom of my heart. Without their help, I would still be trying to type these onto a disk myself!

About the Author

Debbi Throckmorton Stinnett was born and raised in St. Louis, MO. She earned her B.F.A. in fashion design at Stephen's College, Columbia, MO. Debbi worked in the fashion field in St. Louis and Kansas City for many years. Debbi and her husband, Steve, currently live in Springfield, MO. and have two teenage sons, Matt and Blake. Her two teenage sons keep her very busy with their many activities, one being soccer. You might say they are a soccer family devoted to cooking.

Debbi is an active volunteer in the community. She and her husband create gourmet Italian dinners and donate them to two local charities in Springfield. One being the Discovery Center of Springfield which is a children's hands on museum and CASA of Southwest Missouri (Court Appointed Special Advocate). These gourmet dinners involve Debbi and her husband and sons who are called upon occasionally to help! They bring the entire dinner party to the home of the person who bought the dinner at the auction. They have their own menu, which includes several entrees, appetizers and salads of which to choose from. The rest is up to Debbi and Steve, who cook the entire meal, serve it in courses, clean and put the kitchen back together. Coffee and dessert are then served and then Debbi and her crew graciously leave. Needless to say, this impresses all of the guests, and they are already talking about who will buy dinner, at next year's auction. This turns out to be a fun and wonderful way to give back to the community!

Why I Wrote the Book

Five years ago, I decided to write a healthy cookbook. My two sons and husband encouraged me to do this, and in between carpools, soccer games, and many volunteer meetings, I started to create healthy recipes! I asked many of my friends and family members to give me recipes, and then I cooked, analyzed, tasted, and finally with the help of my sons and husband, edited all of the recipes! We think we have chosen the best ones for the book. My family were my best critics! After many endless days and nights of cooking in the kitchen, testing and trying out new recipes, my family gave me their OK on which recipes they liked the best. Without their support, encouragement and love I would have never been able to finish this book. I am truly grateful for their encouragement. They have all been a part of this, and I love them dearly for all of their help.

Table of Contents

Powerful Proteins! 75
Chicken, pork, beef and turkey

Meats pack a lot of protein! We have made these extra healthy for you by cutting the fat and eliminating heavy sauces.

Scrumptious Seafood! 99

From Southwest Missouri Trout to Shrimp Diablo, this seafood is naturally low in fat and packed with Omega 3 fatty acids; seafood is a good choice for healthy meals.

Decadent Desserts! 109

From Strawberry Parfaits to Carrot Cake, these desserts are delectable! You won't miss the butter, I promise!

Dietician

I hope you find this book to be a valuable resource in your pursuit of healthy eating. As a registered dietician, I feel it is important to fix meals for your family that are nutritious, tasty, and can be prepared with minimal time and effort. I think Debbi has done a superb job combining all of these elements in this cookbook.

The recipes in this book that include fat are most often prepared using heart-healthy monounsaturated fats such as olive oil. Incorporating this type of fat into your diet more often, especially when replacing cholesterol-raising saturated fats, is a positive step in reducing cholesterol levels in the blood.

The recipes in this book were analyzed using the computer software Food Processor, and information obtained from food labels. I know you and your family will enjoy the healthy recipes in this book for years to come.

Bon Appetit!

Roxanne Mason RD

Roxanne Mason, RD, CDE

Introduction

You won't believe that you are eating healthy! No dieting here, just easy, healthy meals. The pasta recipes included in this cookbook are REALLY Italian. Recipes from several fine Italian restaurants have been recreated to make them even healthier. We have cut the fat, but not the flavor. These recipes are outstanding and taste fantastic! Your friends will think you are a gourmet cook. This is the only cookbook you will ever need! These recipes are simple to make, yet elegant enough for entertaining. Easy! Easy! Easy!

We have tried to use fresh ingredients in the recipes and tried to make them as healthy as possible without sacrificing taste. We hope you enjoy the book as much as we've enjoyed creating it for you!

Please remember that with all of these recipes, you can be as creative as you want. If you think you should add more of the spices for flavor, try it! On most of the recipes, I play with the ingredients each time I prepare them by adding or omitting different spices or trying a new salsa, cheese, or chip or whatever is new on the market. It seems like every month there are new and easier ingredients available. Experiment!

These are your recipes; I have merely given you a guide to start with. Have fun cooking and entertaining for your family and friends!

It's About
the Way We Eat...

After reading an endless number of fat-free cookbooks, I came to the realization that fat-free is plain awful. We do not need to eat fat-free to lose weight and to be healthy. We need to lower our fat grams and eat smaller portions. We need to change our way of cooking so that we can still have flavor and enjoy eating. After all, it is something we all have to do to maintain our health. We all know that diets simply don't work. We can lose weight on them, sure, but for how long? Invariably most of us gain all of the weight back, and even more only to start on another so called miracle diet that is supposed to be the one that really will work. This whole thing is about the way we eat. It is a total lifestyle change not a diet. We have to eat healthy forever. The only way to this is to learn to cook healthy and to be conscious of what we are eating!

Tips for Eating Out

Eat an apple or drink a glass of skim-milk before you go out if you know you will be tempted to eat a lot of fatty foods.

Always ask for your dressings on the side. Also if you are ordering a pasta with a sauce, ask for your sauce on the side. That way you can add a small amount yourself or look for marinara sauces on the menu. They are usually very low-fat.

Always look for grilled chicken or seafood on the menu. These are the lowest in fat and are usually good as long as you watch what you put on them.

If you are ordering a salad, ask for their low-fat or fat-free dressings and ask them to serve them on the side. Restaurants have become very accommodating and are usually helpful when you ask.

Avoid all fried foods if at all possible.

Read the menu carefully and look for items that are broiled, grilled poached, or steamed. These will usually be a lot lower in fat. Be careful about what you put on them.

Try to avoid vegetables that are in cream sauces or butter.

Always remember butter is a fat!

You can ask for the item you are ordering plain and then you can add lemon juice or whatever condiment they are offering to it yourself.

Most of all, make your choices interesting. Try unusual veggies if they are on the menu.

Don't salt your food. It already has been seasoned in the preparation.

Try to avoid eating bread and butter before your meal is served to you.

If you would like a roll, try not to butter it.

Melba toast's are a good snack to eat while you are waiting for your meal to arrive.

If you truly would like a dessert, try to find one on the menu that has fruit or sorbet with it.

Ingredients to Use
When Possible

Extra light virgin olive oil

Red Wine Vinegar

Fresh minced garlic cloves (if possible)

Balsamic Vinegar

Yellow onion, red onion

Fresh tomatoes (Roma) These are available all year and are tasty.

Low-fat pasta sauces

Low-fat or "free" cream cheese

Fat-free or low-fat sour cream

⅓ less fat cheeses

Low-sodium soups

Low-sodium chicken broth

Fresh herbs if possible (parsley, basil, oregano) They are available all year and are easy to work with and have great flavor.

Pam olive oil spray

Fresh green peppers

Fresh mushrooms

Cooking wines (or any white wines)

Boneless chicken breasts

Black beans (canned variety are easy to keep on hand)

Salsa (many varieties on the market)

Lemons and limes – these make great garnishes

Low-fat tortilla chips

In Their Own Words

Thoughts and feelings from Matt and Blake Stinnett, sons of the author and Steve her husband:

"My mom always has something made for dinner."

"My parents are always trying new things and cooking together. They make cooking fun."

"We love to spend time in our kitchen making up recipes."

"When I walk through the kitchen at dinner time, there seems to always be a new dish being tried or a new spice or something going on!"

"My friends love to eat at my house"

"My mom has probably had *every one* of my friends over for dinner."

"I think my friends are hoping my mom will ask them if they would like to stay for dinner!"

"It seems as though all of us like to cook now, and are always walking by and trying to sneak a new spice in the dish that's cooking!"

"You never know what my Mom and Dad will try next!"

"They are always recreating recipes from restaurants they have been to."

Notes

Awesome Appetizers!

Black Bean Salsa

3	large tomatoes
2	cups black beans drained (I use Progresso)
2	tablespoons extra virgin olive oil
3	garlic cloves minced
2	tablespoons cilantro (fresh)
2	tablespoons fresh chives, chopped fine (heaping)
1	tablespoon fresh lime juice
½	teaspoon ground cumin
¼	teaspoon ground red pepper
¼	teaspoon salt (optional)
¼	teaspoon black pepper (optional)

Peel tomatoes and chop over bowl. Reserve juice and combine next 10 ingredients and juice and refrigerate. Serve with any "baked" tortilla chips. There are several on the market for example: Tostitos, Lays, Guiltless Gourmet, and Doritos. Also great with fresh veggies. These companies all make these chips very low in fat. You can eat several and only be eating 1 gram of fat! *10 servings. 4 tablespoons.*

You may add more black beans to this salsa if you like. It will increase the fat content slightly. Also, you can add more zip with more red pepper. This salsa is so fresh that you won't be able to just eat a little! This gets even better after it is refrigerated.

Calories 48.7
Protein .... 1.44 G
Carbohydrates .... 4.76 G
Dietary Fiber .... 1.65 G
Fat-Total .... 2.99 G
Fat-Saturated .... 0.385 G
Sodium .... 117 Mg
Calories from fat 52%

Avocado Salsa

1	ripe avocado peeled and diced
1	large tomato seeded and chopped
1	tablespoon lemon juice
1	tablespoon white wine vinegar
1	8 ounce package "free" cream cheese (Philadelphia brand)
1	tablespoon oil (olive or canola if possible)
½	cup sliced black olives
1	small can chopped green chilies
2	green onions chopped

In small bowl, toss avocado in lemon juice, set aside. Spread cream cheese either on a plate or a small round glass bowl. In medium bowl, combine olives, chilies, green onions, tomato, and vinegar and oil. Spread evenly over cream cheese. Top with avocado. Serve with either Snackwell crackers or fresh veggies! *19 servings. 3 tablespoons.*

The only real fat in the recipe will be the avocado. You can always omit this.

This makes a very easy tasty salsa! The flavors of the cream cheese make it even better!

Calories	46.9
Protein	2.23 G
Carbohydrates	2.85 G
Dietary Fiber	1.51 G
Fat-Total	3.00 G
Fat-Saturated	0.443 G
Sodium	181 Mg
Calories from fat	57%

Hot Black Bean Dip

2	15 ounce cans black beans
1	medium onion chopped
1	tablespoon extra light virgin olive oil
1-1½	teaspoons cumin
¼-½	teaspoon cayenne pepper
2	tablespoons chili powder
8	ounces ⅓ less fat or fat-free shredded Mozzarella cheese
2	tomatoes chopped
1	16 ounce carton fat-free sour cream

Saute onions and garlic in olive oil. Add chili powder and cayenne and both cans of beans. Mash beans in skillet with a wire whisk. Cook until mixture thickens. Stir in cumin powder and mozzarella cheese. Transfer to glass casserole. Bake at 450° until bubbly. Top with sour cream and tomatoes. Serve with low-fat Tortilla chips. *44 servings. 2-3 tablespoons = 1 serving.*

This is one of those recipes that you can play with. Add chili's to the top if you want, or you can even add a few drops of Tabasco for more zip! Enjoy!

Please remember, if you can not find the exact brand of ingredients, you may substitute with any similar brand that you like or can find.

Calories 38.7
Protein .... 3.04 G
Carbohydrates .... 5.25 G
Dietary Fiber .... 1.30 G
Fat-Total .... 0.539 G
Fat-Mono .... 0.059 G
Sodium .... 111 Mg
Calories from fat 13%

Mexican Pinwheels

4   large flour tortillas
3   packages Philadelphia brand "free" cream cheese
2   small cans chopped green chilies
¼   cup picante sauce or mild salsa
      garlic salt- 4 dashes

Mix all ingredients and spread evenly on each flour tortilla. Roll tortillas and refrigerate for 4 hours or overnight. Slice into 1 inch pinwheels. Secure with toothpicks. Serve with the rest of the salsa as a dip for the pinwheels! *2 pieces of pinwheel= 1 serving. 28 pieces, 14 servings.*

This is a good, easy appetizer for unexpected guests! These ingredients are easy to keep on hand.

Calories 117
Protein .... 9.30 G
Carbohydrates. .... 16.1 G
Dietary Fiber .... 0.853 G
Fat-Total .... 0.911 G
Fat-Saturated .... 0.002 G
Sodium .... 544 Mg
Calories from fat 7%

Crabmeat Mousse

1	10 ½ ounce can Healthy Request tomato soup
1	8 ounce package "free" Philadelphia cream cheese or low-fat brand.
1	large can crabmeat (drained) (8oz)
½	cup chopped green pepper (fine)
½	cup chopped celery (fine)
½	cup green onions (optional)
½	cup sliced green olives
1	cup Hellman's low-fat mayonnaise
1	tablespoon gelatin (Knox) dissolved in ½ cup cold water

Heat soup and cream cheese until warm. Use a wire wisk to mix the cream cheese until smooth. Add gelatin mixture, and rest of ingredients. Pour into a mold sprayed lightly with Pam olive oil spray. Refrigerate until set. I use a fish mold. You can use any design you like. You can garnish the mold with pimento and olives for eyes. *4-6 servings.*

This makes a great summer dinner! Serve over a bed of lettuce. It is also great for an appetizer. Un-mold on a bed of lettuce and serve with your favorite low-fat or fat-free crackers or veggies! Or simply make this your summer entrée along with sliced tomatoes and a veggie! It makes a quick, cold, dinner on a hot summer day!

Calories	238
Protein	17.7 G
Carbohydrates	27.4 G
Dietary Fiber	1.20 G
Fat-Total	5.98
Fat-Saturated	0.485 G
Sodium	1264 Mg
Calories from fats	23%

Spinach Dip

2	10 ounce packages frozen chopped spinach
1	cup Land O' Lakes no-fat sour cream (There are many on the market. I prefer this one.)
1	cup Hellman's Low-Fat Mayonnaise
2	heaping tablespoons dry parsley.
1	.4 ounce package Ranch dry dressing
1	bunch green onions (chopped, including tops)

Defrost spinach in microwave. Squeeze all liquid out until dry. Add all remaining ingredients and chill. The longer this chills, the better the flavor is. If you have time, it's best to make the night before to let the flavors blend. *37 servings. 2 tablespoons.*

The mayonnaise has 1 gram of fat per tablespoon. There are 18 tablespoons in 1 cup. So the whole batch has only 18 total grams of fat! Enjoy!

I serve this dip with Snackwell's crackers. I use the Cracked Pepper or the Classic Golden crackers. Veggies are also great with this and Oh! So Healthy!

Calorie 21.7
Protein .... 0.702 G
Carbohydrates .... 3.65 G
Dietary Fiber .... 0.414 G
Fat-Total .... 0.465 G
Fat-Saturated .... 0.005 G
Sodium .... 82.6 Mg
Calories from fat 19.6%

Spinach Balls

2	10 ounce package frozen chopped spinach, cooked and drained well
2	cups herb seasoned packaged stuffing mix
1	cup fat-free Parmesan cheese
6	egg whites
¾	cup margarine divided ½ fat-free spread (any brand you prefer)
½	cup light butter
	salt and pepper to taste (can omit)

Combine all ingredients, mixing well. Roll into walnut size balls. Place on cookie sheet. Bake 10 minutes at 350°. You can sprinkle Parmesan cheese on just before serving if you prefer. *Sue Throckmorton, Wildwood, Missouri   20 servings. 2 balls.*

These are great to keep on hand in your freezer for unexpected guests or great to serve for parties! My sister in law, Sue has been making these for many years. This is a great, healthy, appetizer. We took out a lot of the fat, and the taste is still as great! This is always one of her favorite appetizers served at every dinner party!

This makes 40-41 balls when I make it, however if you make your balls smaller, it will make more.

Calories 71.5
Protein .... 3.31 G
Carbohydrates .... 9.93 G
Dietary Fiber .... 0.936 G
Fat-Total .... 2.05 G
Fat-Saturated .... 0.009 G
Sodium .... 277 Mg
Calories from fat 26%

Skillet Quesadilla's

1	package flour tortillas, 8 inch size or 99% fat-free burrito size
1	8 ounce package grated Cheddar fat-free cheese
1	8 ounce package grated Mozzarella fat-free cheese
1	can green chilies (chopped)
1	teaspoon cilantro (fresh if possible)

Spray teflon skillet lightly with Pam olive oil spray. Lay tortilla in skillet, add ½ cup cheeses, 2 tablespoons green chilies, and sprinkle with 1 teaspoon dried cilantro. Top with second tortilla and press together gently. On medium heat, cook tortilla until cheeses are melted and then turn and cook other side. Cut into 8 pieces, pizza style with scissors. *8 x 5 = 40 servings.*

These tortillas come in packages of 10. You can make several of these at a time.
Try ⅓ less fat cheese, Kraft shredded cheddar cheese if you prefer. Remember, this will increase your fat grams slightly.

This is an easy appetizer! You can serve with salsa or no fat sour cream for dipping. Remember, you can add other veggies to this: olives, tomatoes, green pepper, etc. These are all fat-free!

Calories 63.9
Protein .... 4.83 G
Carbohydrates .... 10.2 G
Dietary Fiber .... 0.503 G
Fat-Total .... 0.691 G
Fat-Saturated .... 0.001 G
Sodium .... 131 Mg
Calories from fat 9%

Southwest Guacamole

2	ripe avocados peeled and mashed
1	tomato chopped (medium or large)
1	small can chopped green chilies
1	tablespoon fresh lime juice
1-2	chopped green onions or chopped fresh chives (1 bunch)

Peel avocados and mash. Chop tomato including seeds. Add all other ingredients and mix well. Remember, if you are making this ahead of time, leave one of your avocado seeds in, to prevent mixture from turning black. Remove before serving. *16 servings. 2 cups.*

You can add garlic salt or even fresh garlic to make this even more tasty!

Remember: Look for avocados that have turned dark and are soft, but firm to the touch.

Calories 45.9
Protein .... 0.735 G
Carbohydrates .... 3.03 G
Dietary Fiber .... 2.90 G
Fat-Total .... 3.93 G
Fat-Saturated .... 0.662 G
Sodium .... 108 Mg
Calories from fats 70%

24

Pita Grilled Cheese

4   6 inch Pitas
1   16 ounce package (⅓ less fat or no fat brand) grated
      Cheddar cheese
      Pam olive oil spray

Cut a small opening in the top of each pita bread. Fill with shredded cheese. Cook pitas in a preheated skillet sprayed with Pam. Serve immediately. There are many other optional veggies you can add to these. Use you imagination and be creative! *4 servings, 1 pita each.*

These are so easy to make and kids of all ages love them!

Made with 4 ounces fat-free Mozzarella cheese:
Calories 35
Protein .... 40.2 G
Carbohydrates .... 40.6 G
Dietary Fiber .... 0.960 G
Fat-Total .... 0.880 G
Fat-Saturated .... 0.100 G
Sodium .... 1095 Mg
Calories from fats 2%

Made with 4 ounces ⅓ reduced fat Cheddar cheese:
Calories 530
Protein .... 34.6 G
Carbohydrates .... 33.0 G
Dietary Fiber .... 0.960 G
Fat-Total .... 25.2 G
Fat-Saturated .... 16.3 G
Sodium .... 1311 Mg
Calories from fat 46%

Bruschetta

1	thin baguette or loaf of Italian bread, cut into ½" rounds. Sourdough is also good.
	olive oil spray
1	cup "no-fat" or ⅓ less fat grated Mozzarella cheese
1	garlic clove minced (you may use more than one clove)
5-6	medium fresh Roma tomatoes chopped
1	tablespoon olive oil
	chopped fresh basil to taste or may substitute dry (I prefer to use fresh basil; it will enhance the flavor. 5 or 6 leaves. Can add more if you want.)
	may use 4-5 mushrooms sliced
1-2	tablespoon Balsamic vinegar

Spray bread with olive oil, and grill in a toaster oven or on a grill until crust is lightly browned. Mix tomatoes, cheese, garlic, olive oil, vinegar and basil together. Top each bread round with mixture. May heat slightly in oven to melt cheese. You can add many other toppings. Experiment! *24 servings. 1 piece.*

This is one of those fun appetizers you can really change any way you like! This is a wonderful Italian appetizer! Enjoy! This is great served cold over your bread rounds or as a salsa, too.

Calories 63.2
Protein .... 3.35 G
Carbohydrates .... 11.7 G
Dietary Fiber .... 0.608 G
Fat-Total .... 0.215 G
Fat-Saturated .... 0.032 G
Sodium .... 146 Mg
Calories from fat 3%

Pita Pizzas

1   package pitas (whole wheat or white)

1   (16 ounce) jar of your favorite low-fat brand of pasta sauce

1   (16 ounce) package of ⅓ less-fat shredded Cheddar cheese

2   tablespoon shredded fresh basil, or you may use dry

Slice pitas in half and lay on cookie sheet. Top with pasta sauce and cheese. Add basil. Bake at 425° for 8 – 10 minutes. *12 servings, ½ pita each.*

Note: Other optional ingredients you can try: mushrooms, sun-dried tomatoes, red or green bell peppers, Mozzarella cheese, Parmesan cheese, black olives.

Kids love these! They are easy enough for them to make themselves!

We also analyzed this recipe two ways for you to see the difference using fat-free cheese instead of ⅓ less fat cheese. Look at the difference in your fat and sodium content.

Using fat-free cheese:

Calories 152
Protein 15.0g
Carbohydrates 22.0g
Dietary Fiber 1.11g
Fat Total 0.518g
Fat Saturated 0.059g
Sodium 650mg
Calories from fats 3%

Using ⅓ less-fat cheese:

Calories 216
Protein 13.1g
Carbohydrates 19.4g
Dietary Fiber 1.11g
Fat Total 8.62g
Fat Saturated 5.46g
Sodium 722mg
Calories from fats 37%

Sombrero Dip

½   pound diet lean ground beef or ground round
¼   cup chopped onion
¼   cup fancy catsup (I use Brooks because of its tangy flavor)
1 ½   teaspoons chili powder
½   teaspoon salt
2   15 ounce cans dark red kidney beans (do not drain)
½   cup fat-free Cheddar cheese
½   cup chopped green onion including tops
¼   cup green olives, sliced thin

Brown meat and onion. Drain liquid. Add catsup and chili powder. Mash beans in separate bowl with a whisk until completely thick and mushy. Combine all ingredients together in a skillet and heat. Pour in oblong casserole top with cheese, olives, and onions and heat 350° until cheese is melted and bubbly. *45 servings. 2 tablespoons. Claudia Cole-Dallas, Texas*

There are many lower fat tortilla chips out on the market. Experiment with them to see which one you like best. This recipe can easily be doubled, however, I would not double the amount of meat! That will only add to the fat grams! This recipe is always a hit! The original used regular Cheddar cheese! I promise you will copy this recipe for all your guests! They will beg you for this recipe!

Calories 32.0
Protein .... 3.10 G
Carbohydrates .... 3.66 G
Dietary Fiber .... 1.03 G
Fat-Total .... 0.622 G
Fat-Saturated .... 0.171 G
Sodium .... 134 Mg
Calories from fats .... 17 %

Sassy Salads!

Garden Pasta Salad

1	12 ounce R.F garden spirals pasta (carrot spirals and spinach)
1	red bell pepper, chopped
1	green bell pepper, chopped
4-5	chopped green onions including tops
3-4	tablespoon fat-free Parmesan cheese
½	cup Marie fat-free Caesar dressing or any Italian fat-free dressing of your choice or honey dijon dressing.

Cook pasta and drain. Add all vegetables and pasta, then mix in bowl. Add dressing sparingly. You just want to lightly coat the pasta. Add cheese and pepper. Toss. Chill for several hours. Add more dressing before serving, if too dry. *6 servings.*

There are so many options in experimenting with this recipe! You can add as many veggies as you want broccoli, carrots, black olives, etc. You can also experiment with different dressings. Watch out for high sodium content in many of the fat-free dressings. It seems as though there are new dressings out weekly in the supermarkets to try!

Calories 241
Protein 7.72G
Carbohydrates 48.7G
Dietary Fiber 0.953G
Fat-Total 1.04G
Fat-Saturated 0.015G
Sodium 238MG
Calories from fat 4%

Rich and Charlie Salad

1	head Iceberg lettuce
1	head Romaine lettuce (may use red Romaine)
1	14 ounce jar sliced pimentos
1	small or medium red onion sliced very thin into rings
½	cup grated fat-free Parmesan cheese
	fresh pepper to taste and salt if desired

Dressing:

½	cup extra light virgin olive oil (The extra light olive oil tastes better and makes the dressing lighter)
⅓	cup red wine vinegar
	Mix in covered carafe.

Mix lettuce, pimentos, onion and cheese. Right before serving, add dressing only to lightly coat lettuce. You will have dressing left over. You may add more cheese or pepper to taste. *10 servings. 1 cup lettuce.*

This recipe has been used in the Rich and Charlie's restaurant in St. Louis for many years!

This dressing is great to keep on hand! It's easy and tastes great on all of your salads! Keep on hand in the refrigerator, it will stay fresh! I use this basic vinegar and oil dressing for all of my lettuce salads! I left out the artichoke hearts in this recipe, however, if you want added flavor and color, you can use 1 can of artichoke hearts chopped fine...or you may also add a can of hearts of palm.

Calories	162
Protein	3.79 G
Carbohydrates	13.2 G
Dietary-Fiber	6.03 G
Fat Total	11.2G
Fat-Saturated	1.5 G
Sodium	132 Mg
Calories from fat	60%

Curried Chicken Salad

4	cups cooked chicken breast, cut into bite size pieces
2	tablespoons fresh lime juice
1	celery stalk (chopped fine)
4	chopped green onions (including tops)
¼	cup non fat plain yogurt
¼	cup Hellman's low-fat mayonnaise
1- ½	teaspoons curry powder
½	teaspoon cumin

Combine chicken, lime juice, celery, and green onions. In separate bowl combine yogurt, mayonnaise, and spice. Combine both mixtures and coat well. Serve each serving on a bed of lettuce or may be used for sandwiches. *4-6 servings. 1 cup.*

This is one of those recipes that you can really experiment with! You can add different spices to your basic mixture to add a different flavor!

Calories 76.7
Protein .... 8.72 G
Carbohydrates .... 6.83 G
Dietary Fiber .... 0.938 G
Fat-Total .... 1.88 G
Fat-Saturated .... 0.130 G
Sodium .... 134 Mg
Calories from fats 21%

Tuna Salad Stuffed Tomatoes

2	6 oz cans of water packed white albacore tuna, drained and broken apart
½	cup chopped celery
⅓	cup chopped green onions
3	tablespoons Hellman's low-fat mayonnaise
4	large tomatoes (Beefsteak if possible, they are available usually throughout the summer months)
	salt and pepper to taste
1	head of Romaine lettuce (to serve tuna on)

Combine tuna, celery, green onions and mayonnaise. Salt and pepper to taste. Slice tomatoes to create a star, fill with tuna salad and serve on a bed of lettuce. *4 servings. ½ cup tuna.*

You may add other ingredients to your salad if you wish. Other options could be, sweet pickle relish, green or red pepper, and or olives.

This makes a pretty luncheon dish! It is also great for a light dinner!

Calories 158
Protein .... 25.7 G
Carbohydrates .... 9.86 G
Dietary Fiber .... 2.26 G
Fat-Total .... 1.61 G
Fat-Saturated .... 0.195 G
Sodium .... 424 Mg
Calories from fats 9%

Summer Veggie Salad

2	large tomatoes chopped in chunks
½	red onion (chopped)
1	yellow pepper cut into chunks
1	red pepper cut into chunks
1	green pepper cut into chunks
1	cucumber chopped into chunks (you may peel or leave the skin on)

Dressing:

¼	cup extra virgin olive oil (always use light)
⅓	cup red wine vinegar
3	garlic cloves, minced
3	tablespoon fresh basil, chopped
	salt and pepper optional
	capers optional

Chop all vegetables and mix together in bowl. Wisk dressing together in separate bowl and pour over vegetables and mix. Refrigerate until ready to serve. *6-8 servings. Sandy Webster-Charlotte, North Carolina*

This makes a beautiful salad that can be served at a Bar- B-Que or elegant enough to serve at a dinner party. This is a great dish to take to any gathering, just make sure you have the recipe handy to give out! When my sister-in-law served this salad, I had to have the recipe for the book!

Calories 121
Protein .... 1.49 G
Carbohydrates .... 9.91 G
Dietary Fiber .... 2.35 G
Fat-Total .... 9.37 G
Fat-Saturated .... 1.27 G
Sodium .... 6.90 Mg
Calories from fats 65%

Ambrosia Salad

1	16 ounce package small marshmallows
1	small jar maraschino cherries (sliced in half)
1	can mandarin oranges (drained)
1	16 ounce Dannon plain yogurt
1	15- ¾ ounce can pineapple tidbits (drained, save liquid)
½	pound non-fat Land O' Lakes sour cream (if you can not find this brand, you may substitute.)

Mix all ingredients together and add some of your juice from your cherries for color and sweetness, also use some of your left over pineapple juice to taste. Add the amount of sour cream you want to taste depending on how creamy you want this. *8-10 servings. 1 cup. Suzy Hamelink- Charlotte, North Carolina*

When my sister-in-law served this, I couldn't believe it was basically fat-free. It is a beautiful salad, and you will never believe it's so low-fat! Most of all, you won't believe how great this is! This is on our Easter table every year!

Calories 263
Protein .... 6.29 G
Carbohydrates .... 59.5 G
Dietary Fiber .... 1 .75 G
Fat-Total .... 1.27 G
Fat-Saturated 0.62
Sodium .... 111 Mg
Calories from fats .... 4 %

Mandarin Orange Jell-O Salad

2	small boxes orange Jell-O
1	large can mandarin oranges (drained)
1	small can frozen orange juice (6oz.)
1	medium can crushed pineapple
1	small container Cool Whip Lite
1	small box instant lemon pudding

Mix orange Jell-O with 2 cups boiling water. Add mandarin oranges, pineapple and orange juice. Pour into oblong glass casserole dish.

Refrigerate until set. Mix Cool Whip and lemon pudding (add skim milk per directions on pudding). Frost top of set jello with topping. Serve after jell-o in completely jelled. This makes a very refreshing, pretty salad that is perfect for a summer Barbecue! *12 servings.*

Calories 175
Protein .... 1.44 G
Carbohydrates .... 36.6 G
Dietary Fiber .... 0.964 G
Fat-Total .... 2.43 G
Fat-Saturated .... 2.37 G
Sodium .... 95.1 Mg
Calories from fat 13%

Cucumber Salad

1	large red onion, sliced into thin rings
3-4	medium peeled cucumbers, sliced into ¼ inch slices
3	large tomatoes, sliced
6	cups of water
½	cup red wine vinegar or to taste
2	tablespoons salt

Combine all ingredients and let marinate several hours if possible. Serve as a salad in a pretty glass bowl. *10-12 servings. Doris Stinnett- St. Louis, Missouri.*

This is a favorite of my mother-in-law's! It is a beautiful salad for any summer occasion! You can omit the cucumbers or the tomatoes and just serve one or the other with the onion.

Calories 28.1
Protein .... 1.05 G
Carbohydrates .... 6.64 G
Dietary Fiber .... 1.89 G
Fat-Total .... 0.276 G
Fat-Saturated .... 0.055 G
Sodium .... 1169 Mg
Calories from fats 7%

Spicy Caesar Salad

Dressing:
3	cloves fresh garlic, minced
½	cup low-fat mayo
2	tablespoons red wine vinegar
1	tablespoon white wine vinegar
1	tablespoon Dijon mustard
2	tablespoons anchovy paste
1	teaspoon fresh ground pepper
	Cajun seasoning

Croutons:
2	cups sourdough bread, cut into bite size cubes
	Pam olive oil cooking spray
	Cajun seasoning (dash)

Salad:
2	hearts of romaine – torn
⅓	cup shredded Parmesan cheese

Preheat oven to 400 degrees. Place bread cubes on cooking sheet (stone is better), and spray with cooking spray. Sprinkle with Cajun seasoning to taste. Bake for 10-15 minutes or until golden brown.

Combine all ingredients for dressing in food processor. Refrigerate before serving.

Toss lettuce, cheese, dressing and croutons in large bowl. Serve and enjoy! *6 servings, 1 cup each. Melissa Hamelink-Charlotte, North Carolina.*

Calories 108.68
Protein .... 4.9 G
Carbohydrates .... 13.628 G
Dietary Fiber .... 1.295 G
Fat Total .... 3.908 G
Fat-Saturated 1.214G
Sodium .... 467 Mg
Calories from fat 32%

Vigorous Vegetables!

Ragin' Cajun French Fries

4-5	potatoes (any kind)
3-4	egg whites
	dash of water
	McCormick Cajun Chicken Seasoning to taste
	Pam olive oil spray

Slice or cut potatoes any way you like. I leave the skin on. You can also use a "potato twister" if you want curly fries. Mix egg whites and water in a small bowl. Dip potatoes in mixture. Arrange on cookie sheet sprayed with Pam. Generously sprinkle cajun seasoning over potatoes. Bake at 425° for approximately 45 minutes, turning once. These fries will be nice and crispy. *4 servings.*

This can almost pass for the great fast food curly fries! (I said almost!)

Calories 265
Protein .... 8.75 G
Carbohydrates .... 57.7 G
Dietary Fiber .... 5.29 G
Fat-Total .... 0.225 G
Fat-Saturated .... 0.058 G
Sodium .... 203 Mg
Calories from fats 1%

Cheesy Mashed Potatoes

8-10	potatoes (either red or Idaho)
1	8 ounce package Neufachel cream cheese
1	16 ounce "Land O' Lakes" fat-free sour cream
½	cup skim milk
½	cup grated Cheddar cheese (you can use Healthy Choice fat-free or Kraft ⅓ less fat)
1-2	green onion chopped (you can add more depending on your preference)
	garlic salt to taste

Peel and boil potatoes until tender when pierced with a fork. Drain and then mash, adding milk, cream cheese, and sour cream and green onion. Garlic salt to taste. Pour into a casserole dish sprayed with Pam or olive oil. Spread cheese on top and bake at 350° for 45 minutes. *9 servings. Sue Throckmorton, Wildwood, Missouri*

This makes an easy company dish! This recipe is a favorite of my brother and sister-in-law. They all love this and it has become one of my family's favorite, too! By using fat-free ingredients, we have taken a lot of the fat out, but believe me, we haven't taken the flavor out!

If you use fat-free cheese on this, watch for hardening. This cheese gets very hard when cooked too long and also as it cooks. You can use ½ fat-free cheese and mix some of the ⅓ less-fat together to keep it from hardening. Also, if you can not find Land O' Lakes Fat-Free Sour Cream, you may substitute another brand, but please taste before using, as some of the other brands have a terrible taste!

We analyzed this two ways for you to see the difference between the two cheeses. Made with .056 cup fat-free Cheddar cheese:

Calories	265
Protein	11.0 G
Carbohydrates	41.6 G
Dietary Fiber	2.97 G
Fat-Total	6.11 G
Fat-Saturated	3.78 G
Sodium	240 Mg
Calories from fats	21%

Made with .222 ounces ⅓ reduced-fat Cheddar:

Calories	276
Protein	10.6 G
Carbohydrates	41.2 G
Dietary Fiber	2.97 G
Fat-Total	7.46 G
Fat-Saturated	4.68 G
Sodium	250 Mg
Calories from fats	24%

Potatoes on the Grill

	Idaho or red potatoes (1 per person)
1-2	tablespoons Kraft fat-free Parmesan cheese
	garlic salt to taste
¼-1	teaspoon oregano
1-2	spray of Pam olive oil spray

Slice potatoes in ¼ inch slices, keeping together (keep skin on) on a square of aluminum foil. Spread potatoes and add cheese and spices in between. Spray Pam olive oil spray on potatoes. Wrap in foil tightly and cook on grill along side your meat. You can put these in the oven on 400° for 45 minutes. *1 potato per person.*

You can add many other ingredients to these, such as green onions, fat-free cheeses or any other spices you may prefer. These make an easy side dish for any Bar B Que without the fat!

Calories 416
Protein .... 9.33 G
Carbohydrates .... 94.9 G
Dietary Fiber .... 7.92 G
Fat-Total .... 0.337 G
Fat-Saturated .... 0.088 G
Sodium .... 392 Mg
Calories from fats 1%

Pan Fried Potatoes

½-1   teaspoons extra virgin olive oil
6-8   red potatoes unpeeled and diced
½   small onion chopped fine (can add more if desired)
       black pepper to taste
       lite salt (if you prefer)

Heat olive oil in non stick skillet. Add onions and potatoes. Cook on medium heat stirring frequently 10-15 minutes. Cover and cook 20-30 minutes, turning frequently then remove lid. Cook 10-15 minutes, or until lightly browned. Sprinkle with black pepper. Can salt lightly. *6 servings.*

Fried potatoes are usually fried in lots of oil. This way they are light and still very flavorful!
These are great served with any kind of fish!

Calories 200
Protein .... 3.64 G
Carbohydrates .... 39.3 G
Dietary Fiber .... 3.73 G
Fat-Total. .... 3.55 G
Fat-Saturated .... 0.499 G
Sodium .... 104 Mg
Calories from fats 16%

43

Healthy Baked Potatoes

1	Idaho potato
2	tablespoons Land O' Lakes fat-free sour cream
1	tablespoon chopped green onions
2	tablespoons shredded cheese (fat-free Healthy Choice or ⅓ less fat)

Wash and pierce potato with fork. Bake at 450° for 1 hour. Split in half and add all other ingredients. Salsa is also good on these. *1 potato per person.*

This makes a healthy lunch or dinner when you are in a hurry and don't want to go to the trouble of cooking!

Made with 2 tablespoons fat-free Cheddar:

Calories 425
Protein .... 14.4 G
Carbohydrates .... 92.4 G
Dietary Fiber .... 8.07 G
Fat-Total .... 0.349 G
Fat-Saturated .... 0.090 G
Sodium .... 67.9 Mg
Calories from fats .... 1 %

Made with .5 ounces ⅓ reduced-fat Cheddar:

Calories 448
Protein .... 13.5 G
Carbohydrates .... 91.4 G
Dietary Fiber .... 8.07 G
Fat-Total .... 3.39 G
Fat-Saturated .... 2.11 G
Sodium .... 189 Mg
Calories from fats 7%

Fresh Green Beans

1-1 ½ pounds fresh green beans washed and snapped in half
2-3   garlic cloves minced
10-12   fresh mushrooms sliced
1   tablespoon extra virgin olive oil

Combine all ingredients in a deep frying pan. Add small amount of water. Cover and gently steam until tender. Pepper to taste. *6 servings. ½ cup.*

If you like onion in your beans, you can add chopped onion with your garlic. This is a very simple vegetable to make and always comes out great!

Calories 76.1
Protein .... 3.74 G
Carbohydrates .... 12.1 G
Dietary Fiber .... 3.96 G
Fat-Total .... 2.71 G
Fat-Saturated .... 0.379 G
Sodium .... 9.46 Mg
Calories from fat 28%

California Stir Fried Green Beans

½   pound fresh green beans, sliced diagonally into 2 inch pieces
¼   pound fresh carrots sliced diagonally into 2 inch pieces
1   tablespoon extra virgin olive oil
2   garlic cloves crushed
¼   cup chicken broth
1   teaspoon honey
1   teaspoon sherry
1   tablespoon soy sauce
     ginger to taste

After washing beans and carrots, slice diagonally. Heat oil in wok or large frying pan. Add garlic, ginger, beans, and carrots. Stir fry adding chicken broth. Cover and cook on medium heat for 2 minutes. *4-6 servings. ½ cup. Jill Seagrave-Springfield, Missouri.*

This is a pretty summer veggie that is great for all of your cookouts!

Calories	56.0
Protein	1.33 G
Carbohydrates	6.73 G
Dietary Fiber	1.89 G
Fat-Total	2.78 G
Fat-Saturated	0.383 G
Sodium	160 Mg
Calories from fats	44%

Lemon Asparagus

1 ½	pounds fresh asparagus spears
1	egg beaten
⅓	cup light margarine
2	teaspoons sugar
½	teaspoon cornstarch
½	cup fresh lemon juice

Snap off tough ends of asparagus and wash thoroughly in colander. Cook asparagus in a small amount of water until crisp/tender. Drain. Arrange in serving dish. Combine egg, margarine, sugar, and cornstarch on low heat. Cook until margarine is melted and cornstarch starts to thicken. Add lemon juice. Cook, stirring constantly until thickened. Pour over asparagus. *4 servings.*

This is an easy vegetable, especially for company. This sauce is very similar to Hollandaise but a little lighter on the fat grams! Asparagus is especially good in the spring, when stalks are thin. This recipe can be experimented with using partially fat-free margarine and regular margarine.

Calories 139
Protein .... 6.87 G
Carbohydrates .... 11.3 G
Dietary Fiber .... 2.48 G
Fat-Total .... 9.64 G
Fat-Saturated .... 0.484 G
Sodium .... 137 Mg
Calories from fats 54%

Cauliflower Cheese Casserole

1	head cauliflower
⅓	cup Fleismann's fat-free low-calorie spread
15	fat-free saltine crackers, plus 4 more after you add 2nd cup of milk to thicken
2	cups skim milk
¾	pound Velveeta light cheese (2 pound box = 3 fat grams per 1 ounce) salt and white pepper to taste

Trim leaves from cauliflower. Put in colander over a pot with a small amount of water. Steam with foil over for a tent until cauliflower can be pierced with a fork and is not hard. Just to get it softened a little. Do not cook. After steaming, cut or break into florets and lay in casserole dish. Combine Fleismann's spread and 15 crackers crushed in pan on medium heat. Add 1 cup of milk continuing to stir. Mixture should boil on medium heat. Add 4 more crackers and 2nd cup of milk. Mixture will thicken again. Slowly add cubes of cheese until melted. Add white pepper. You may add more for extra flavor. Pour cheese mixture over cauliflower. Bake at 350° uncovered for 45 minutes. *10 servings. ½ cup. Helen Behymer- Webster Groves, Missouri.*

This recipe is a family favorite of my husband's grandmother and is on our table every Thanksgiving!

I have taken a lot of the fat out by using skim milk and light Velveeta cheese.

Calories	132
Protein	10.6 G
Carbohydrates	10.0 G
Dietary Fiber	1.15 G
Fat-Total	3.81 G
Fat-Saturated	2.50 G
Sodium	650 Mg
Calories from fats	26%

Broiled Summer Tomatoes

4	large fresh tomatoes
½	cup bread crumbs (may use seasoned for more flavor)
1-2	tablespoons olive oil (I prefer to use 1 tablespoon)
¼	cup fat-free Parmesan cheese
1	teaspoon oregano
	salt and pepper to taste

Cut center out of each tomato and scoop out a little from each. Mix bread crumbs, cheese, olive oil, salt, pepper, and oregano. Fill the hollow with the crumb mixture. Arrange on a broiler pan. Place under broiler for 15 minutes on low heat. *4 servings. 1 tomato.*

This makes a nice summer veggie, especially with home grown tomatoes!

Calories 134
Protein .... 3.84 G
Carbohydrates .... 20.5 G
Dietary Fiber .... 2.36 G
Fat-Total .... 4.57 G
Fat-Saturated .... 0.521 G
Sodium .... 339 Mg
Calories from fat .... 30 %

Fresh Zucchini
Italian Style

2	medium zucchini (may use green, yellow, or both)
½	onion chopped
1	tablespoon extra virgin olive oil
½-1	tablespoon oregano
1	8 ounce can crushed tomatoes (these can be substituted for whole peeled tomatoes)

Slice zucchini and onion and saute in olive oil. Add tomatoes and oregano. Simmer until cooked. Do not over cook. You will want the zucchini to still have a slight crunch to it. Serve immediately. This does not need any extra salt. *4 servings.*

Please remember, you can modify this recipe to your liking. Be creative! If you do not like as much tomato, then only use half of the amount listed! I have found that in most of my recipes, there is no need to add salt! Many of the spices add more flavor than salt!

Calories 59.8
Protein .... 1.57 G
Carbohydrates .... 6.41 G
Dietary Fiber .... 1.66 G
Fat-Total .... 3.69 G
Fat-Saturated .... 0.515 G
Sodium .... 94.4 Mg
Calories from fat 51%

Bold Beans!

White Bean Soup

1	(16 ounce) package great white northern beans
1	onion chopped
2-3	carrots, chopped (may use more if you prefer)
1	(16 ounce) can crushed tomatoes
3	garlic cloves minced
	salt and pepper to taste

Rinse beans in colander and then soak beans overnight or early in the day in two inches of water in a large stockpot. Add onion, carrot, garlic and tomatoes. Simmer on low several hours. Soup will get thick. You can add more water as it thickens if you prefer. *12 servings. 1 cup.*

Note: This is a recipe my husband used to make in college; I had never had it before, and he's been making it for me ever since. He, of course, made it with a large ham hock! And lots of red pepper flakes.

This is your basic white bean soup without the ham hock. It is so easy to make and is a hearty meal served with bread. For extra spice, add several drops of Tabasco sauce. This will really add flavor.

Calories 146
Protein 8.66g
Carbohydrates 27.8g
Dietary Fiber 2.03g
Fat Total 0.586g
Fat Saturated 0.136g
Sodium 70.7mg
Calories from fats 3%

Red Beans and Rice

2	cans dark red kidney beans (drained a little)
4	cups water, divided
1	cup chopped onion
1	cup chopped green bell pepper
3	garlic cloves; peeled and minced
¾	teaspoon dried oregano
½	teaspoon dried thyme
1	teaspoon ground black pepper
½	teaspoon crushed red pepper
1	bay leaf
½	pound Healthy Choice low-fat polska kielbasa (This comes two to a package. I just slice up one and freeze the other for the next time or if you prefer more sausage you use the whole package. It will not increase your fat that much)
2	cup rice, uncooked
12	ounce crushed tomatoes (part of)

Place beans, 2-cups of water, onion, bell pepper and garlic in a large saucepot; bring to a boil. Reduce heat to medium. Cook, uncovered, stirring occasionally for 30 minutes. Add oregano, thyme, black pepper, red pepper, bay leaf, sausage and remaining 2 cups of water. Cook 30 minutes, simmering gently. Remove and discard bay leaf. Add in rice. Cover and cook 30 more minutes or until rice is tender. At this time, I usually add part of a 12 ounce can of crushed tomatoes. This gives color and a slight tomato taste. This is optional. Also if you prefer your beans on top of your rice, you can omit the 2-cups of water and just cook your rice separately. *6 servings.*

This has a wonderful flavor and is so healthy to eat! This is also good the next day re-heated.

Calories	92	
Protein	18.2	G
Carbohydrates	75.7	G
Dietary Fiber	7.08	G
Fat-Total	1.69	G
Fat-Saturated	0.494	G
Sodium	704	Mg
Calories from fats	4%	

Black Beans and Rice

3	cans black beans rinsed and drained
3	garlic cloves minced
2	cup low sodium chicken broth
2	cup long grain rice
1	small onion chopped fine (1 cup)
2	teaspoon extra virgin olive oil
1	16 ounce can crushed tomatoes or you may substitute a can of whole tomatoes cut up without the juice
2	tablespoon red wine vinegar (to taste)
¼	teaspoon cayenne
1	tablespoon cilantro

Bring rice and chicken broth to a boil and simmer covered, until rice is tender and liquid is absorbed approximately 20 minutes. While rice is cooking, saute onion and garlic in olive oil until tender. Add black beans, tomatoes and cayenne. Simmer for 5-10 minutes. Add vinegar to taste and stir in cilantro. You may add your rice and bean mixture together or you may serve the bean mixture over the rice. *5-6 servings. 1 cup.*

This has great flavor and is so easy to make.

Calories	279
Protein	12.0 G
Carbohydrates	49.9 G
Dietary Fiber	3.83 G
Fat-Total	3.04 G
Fat-Saturated	0.295 G
Sodium	609 Mg
Calories from fats	10%

Picnic Basket
Baked Beans

4	11 ounce cans pork and beans
½	cup molasses (can add more to make thicker)
⅓	cup packed brown sugar (golden brown)
⅓	cup barbecue sauce (I use a sweet kind-Curly's is a brand that I am able to find. Any sweet style will work.)
½-1	teaspoon yellow mustard

Combine beans and all other ingredients in a oblong glass casserole dish. Bake at 325 ° for 1-2 hours. The longer you bake these, the thicker they become. *8-10 or more servings. ½ cup.*

Calories 206
Protein .... 6.77 G
Carbohydrates .... 42.8 G
Dietary Fiber .... 6.91 G
Fat-Total .... 2.05 G
Fat-Saturated .... 0.720 G
Sodium .... 501 Mg
Calories from fats 9%

Lotta Bean Chili

½	lb. lean ground beef or turkey
1	green pepper, chopped
1	yellow onion, chopped
1	large can Brooks chili hot beans (there are several different kinds on the market)
4	cans dark red kidney beans (drained)
4	tablespoon chili powder (you can add more if you prefer)
3	tablespoon cumin
1	29 ounce large can crushed tomatoes (you can use whole if you prefer)
1	can tomato sauce

Brown meat onion and green pepper. Drain liquid. Transfer to large pot and add beans, tomatoes, chili powder and cumin. Simmer covered on low for 30 minutes. This is better the longer you cook it. *8-10 servings. 1 cup.*

You can play with the amount of beans and tomato sauce. Add more if you like. It will not increase your fat grams! This is great for cold winter suppers! Serve with sourdough bread or cornbread and you've got a great hearty meal! If you prefer less bean in your chili, you can cut down the amount.

Calories	317
Protein	36.6 G
Carbohydrate	36.8 G
Dietary Fiber	11.4 G
Fat-Total	2.46 G
Fat-Saturated	0.187 G
Sodium	1236 Mg
Calories from fats	7%

Lentil Chili

⅓	cup extra virgin olive oil
1	medium chopped onion
2	cloves garlic minced
1	medium carrot, chopped
7	cup water
⅓	cup tomato paste
2	cup brown lentils rinsed and drained
1	green pepper chopped
1	sweet red pepper chopped
1	19-ounce can red kidney beans drained
1	cup garbanzo beans
2	cup crushed tomatoes
⅓	cup chili powder
4	teaspoon cumin
¼	teaspoon red pepper
	lightly salt

Heat olive oil and saute onion, garlic, and carrot until onions are clear. Add water, tomato paste, tomatoes, lentils, peppers and beans. Stir and then add tomatoes and spices. Boil and then simmer for 45-60 minutes . You can increase spices to taste before serving. Don't over cook, you don't want your lentils mushy. You can sprinkle fat-free Parmesan cheese on top if desired. *10 servings.*

This is a healthy, hearty chili! Great for those cold winter nights! It's loaded with fiber!

Calories	312
Protein	17.1 G
Carbohydrates	45.1 G
Dietary Fiber	10.1 G
Fat-Total	8.71 G
Fat-Saturated	1.24 G
Sodium	410 G
Calories from fats	24%

Black Bean Burritos

6	small (8") low-fat flour tortillas
1	tablespoon olive oil
½	cup chopped onion
3	garlic cloves, minced
½-1	teaspoon cumin
⅛	teaspoon black pepper
	Red pepper flakes to taste (⅛ teaspoon)
1	(15ounce) can black beans, rinsed and drained
½-1	cups diced, fresh mango. (This would equal 1 mango, or you may use mangos that are already peeled in a jar, available in the refrigerated section of your grocery store. Do not use the juice.)
1	tablespoon light brown sugar
1	tablespoon fresh lemon juice
½	cup low-fat cheddar cheese
1	cup fat-free sour cream (Land O Lakes makes a tasty version)
½-1	cups diced Roma tomatoes (These are good all year long).
½	cup fresh cilantro, chopped

Sauté onion in olive oil until clear. Add garlic, cumin, black beans, black pepper and red pepper flakes. Heat thoroughly. In a separate small pan, heat brown sugar, lemon juice and diced mango until soft and juicy.

You may warm tortillas in a 350 degree oven or in the microwave for a few seconds. Be sure to cover them.

Place divided bean mixture down center of each tortilla and top with cheese. Roll burritos and place seam side down in glass casserole dish. Heat thoroughly in 350 degree oven for 25 minutes. 6 servings, 1 tortilla each.

To serve, top each burrito with sour cream, mango mixture, tomatoes and top with cilantro.

This makes a beautiful dish to serve! You can serve these garnishes on the side if you prefer.

Calories 328
Protein 13.7G
Carbohydrates .... 56.743 G
Dietary Fiber .... 7.111 G
Fat Total 5.9G
Fat-Saturated 1.174G
Sodium .... 503 MG
Calories from fat 16%

Crazy For Carbs!

Sun Dried Tomato Bowtie Pasta

1	package Sonoma dried tomatoes (found in canned tomato section may substitute for any other brand)
1	tablespoon olive oil
1	small chopped onion
3	garlic cloves crushed
1	cup white wine (you may substitute with cooking wine)
3	teaspoon basil (fresh is preferred, if not use ½-1 tsp. chopped)
¼	teaspoon cracked red pepper
1	package bowtie pasta (16 ounce)
1	28 ounce can crushed tomato
1	teaspoon sugar (right before serving to cut tomato taste)

Saute onions and garlic in olive oil. Add wine and reduce liquid simmering for 10-15 minutes. After soaking 12-15 dried tomatoes in warm water for 5 minutes, chop and add to wine mixture. Turn up heat to combine flavors. Add crushed tomatoes, basil, red pepper and sugar. Simmer 20-30 minutes. Serve mixed together with bowtie pasta garnished with Parmesan cheese. *6 servings.*

Did you know that it takes 17 pounds of fresh tomatoes to make one pound of dried tomatoes? This adds rich intense tomato flavor! And it makes a rich, thick sauce! Remember, experiment with spices. You can add more pepper if you want your sauce extra spicy! Be creative!

```
Calories .................................. 416
Protein ............................. 14.1 G
Carbohydrates .................. 75.2 G
Dietary Fiber .................... 4.73 G
Fat-Total .......................... 3.92 G
Fat-Saturated ................. 0.359 G
Sodium ............................ 345 Mg
Calories from fats ................. 9%
```

Tomato and Black Bean Pasta

3	large chopped tomatoes
¾	cup black beans (drained)
2	tablespoon extra virgin olive oil
3	garlic cloves minced
2	tablespoon cilantro
1	tablespoon lime juice
½	teaspoon ground cumin
¼	teaspoon ground red pepper
¼	teaspoon salt
¼	teaspoon black pepper
16	ounce vermicelli pasta

Peel tomatoes and chop. Reserve juice and combine next 9 ingredients in skillet gently cooking until tomatoes are thoroughly cooked and sauce has simmered for several minutes. Cook pasta al denté, drain and add to serving bowl. Top with mixture, sprinkle with fat-free Parmesan cheese and serve. *6 - 1 cup servings.*

Calories 361
Protein .... 11.7 G
Carbohydrates .... 63.9 G
Dietary Fiber .... 2.74 G
Fat-Total .... 6.24 G
Fat-Saturated .... 0.641 G
Sodium .... 270 Mg
Calories from fats 16%

Old Fashioned Spaghetti Sauce

½	pound diet ground beef
1	medium onion, chopped
3	large garlic cloves, whole
1	green pepper, chopped
1	12 ounce tomato paste (use as needed, might have small amount left)
1	15 ounce can tomato sauce
1	28 ounce can whole tomatoes (you can chop if you like)
2	teaspoon oregano
¼	teaspoon thyme
½	teaspoon rosemary
¼	teaspoon marjoram

Saute meat, onion and green pepper until pepper is soft. Drain any juice from pan. Transfer to larger pot, add tomato paste, tomato sauce and whole tomatoes. Mix well, and then add garlic cloves and your spices. Cover and simmer for several hours. The longer this sauce cooks, the better the flavor is. Serve over spaghetti or mostaciolli pasta. You can add a small can of water to this sauce so it's not too thick. *8 servings. ½ cup.*

This is a great sauce to freeze. You will always have it on hand when you don't have time to cook! If you like mushrooms, you add a small can or fresh to this sauce. The longer this sauce simmers, the better it is!

By using lean beef, you have greatly reduced your fat grams!

Calories 148
Protein .... 11.7 G
Carbohydrates .... 19.3 G
Dietary Fiber .... 4.27 G
Fat-Total .... 3.99 G
Fat-Saturated .... 1.31 G
Sodium .... 838 Mg
Calories from fats 22%

Pasta Con Broccoli

1	pound fresh broccoli
1	cup Campbell's Healthy Request chicken broth
1	cup skim milk
2	tablespoon white wine or cooking wine
2	garlic cloves crushed
¾	cup tomato sauce
16	ounce cavatelli pasta or shell pasta
4	tablespoon fat-free Parmesan cheese
3	tablespoon cornstarch dissolved in 3 tablespoon water
	salt and pepper to taste

Wash and cut ends off broccoli and lightly steam (set aside do not cook). In sauce pan, combine milk, chicken broth, garlic and wine. Heat on medium. Slowly, add your cornstarch mixture. The sauce will thicken; if you want it thicker, add more cornstarch mixture. Add tomato sauce and Parmesan cheese. Cut broccoli into florets and add to mixture. Prepare pasta and add to sauce. You may add more Parmesan cheese for flavor. *8 servings. 1 cup.*

This Pasta Con Broccoli has a nice flavor minus the whipping cream!

Calories 256
Protein .... 10.5 G
Carbohydrates .... 50.3 G
Dietary Fiber .... 2.26 G
Fat-Total .... 1.24 G
Fat-Saturated .... 0.074 G
Sodium .... 287 Mg
Calories from fats 4%

Fresh Basil
Marinara Sauce

2	garlic cloves crushed
1	tablespoon extra light virgin olive oil
1	small yellow onion, chopped
¾	cup white wine (any kind will do or you may substitute with white cooking wine)
1	16 ounce can diced tomatoes
1-2	tablespoons basil (fresh) (you can substitute with dry)
⅛	teaspoon red pepper flakes (you can add more at end if you like your sauce spicier)
1	teaspoon sugar (be very careful not to add too much)
1-2	teaspoons tomato paste to thicken sauce at the end
1	pound vermicelli pasta cooked al denté

Sauté onion and garlic in olive oil. Do not brown garlic. Sauté only until onion is clear. Add wine and simmer until wine is reduced. It will have a slightly thicker consistency and be slightly less liquid in the pan. Add crushed tomatoes, basil and red pepper flakes. Add paste. Continue to simmer for a few minutes so flavors can blend. Add 1 teaspoon sugar at end. Serve over vermicelli cooked al denté in a big pasta bowl and sprinkle with Parmesan cheese. *6 servings. ½ cup.*

A lot of recipes that call for fresh garlic sauteed, request to remove garlic after cook. This is optional. Be sure not to burn or overcook the garlic.

This is so easy and quick. This is just as great with bowtie pasta!

Calories	334
Protein	9.97 G
Carbohydrates	59.8 G
Dietary Fiber	1.30 G
Fat-Total	3.76 G
Fat-Saturated	0.340 G
Sodium	125 Mg
Calories from fats	11%

Chicken Angelina

4   boneless skinless breasts cut into ¼ inch strips
2   tablespoon extra virgin olive oil
2   garlic cloves crushed
1   tablespoon butter
½ cup chopped onion
1   cup chicken broth
1   tablespoon oregano
2   tablespoon dried parsley
½ teaspoon crushed red pepper
4   Roma tomatoes diced
1   bunch fresh spinach (remove stems and wash)
¼ cup Parmesan cheese
      salt and pepper to taste
1   pound vermicelli or thin spaghetti

Saute onion, garlic, and chicken pieces in olive oil. Add butter chicken broth, and tomatoes. Bring to a boil, and reduce broth. Add spices, red pepper, parsley, oregano and continue to simmer for 10 minutes. Boil pasta until it is al denté (which is firm to taste) Then add to your sauce and toss with fresh spinach. Continue to cook on low until spinach is cooked down. Sprinkle with Parmesan cheese and serve immediately. *4 servings.*

This recipe comes from one of our favorite Italian restaurants in St. Louis. We loved this recipe so much, that we added it to the book, and you will be glad we did!

Calories 776
Protein .... 52 G
Carbohydrates .... 93 G
Dietary Fiber .... 3 G
Fat Total .... 19 G
Fat Saturated .... 5 G
Sodium .... 609 Mg
Calories from fats 22%

Chicken Manicotti Florentine

6	ounce cooked chicken breast (chopped)
½	medium onion, chopped
1	teaspoon garlic, crushed
2	teaspoon fresh basil (or use dry)
1	teaspoon Italian herb seasoning
1	package frozen, chopped spinach, thawed and squeezed
1½	cups spaghetti sauce (can use Healthy Choice or any other brand on market)
6	ounce sliced fresh mushrooms
2	tablespoon white wine or white cooking wine if you prefer
8	ounce lite cottage cheese
10	manicotti shell cooked and drained (al denté)
4	tablespoon Parmesan cheese (I use Kraft fat-free or Weight Watchers)

Spray large skillet with PAM olive oil spray. Saute onion, garlic, basil and herb seasoning for 2 minutes. Add spinach and chicken. Blend and cook for 2 minutes. Remove from heat and set aside, cook mushrooms and wine in separate pan for five minutes. Drain cottage cheese and add to chicken/spinach mixture. Carefully stuff each manicotti and place seam down side by side in glass casserole dish. Pour sauce over and sprinkle with Parmesan cheese. Bake 30 minutes at 350°. Serve with crusty sourdough bread and a green salad. *5 servings. 2 manicotti noodles.*

This takes a little more time to make, but it's definitely worth it!

Calories	425
Protein	25.2 G
Carbohydrates	73.8 G
Dietary Fiber	3.68 G
Fat-Total	2.67 G
Fat-Saturated	0.337 G
Sodium	559 Mg
Calories from fats	6%

Turkey Bolognese

1	16 ounce jar Healthy Choice pasta sauce (you may choose from several brands on the market)
½	pound ground turkey breast
2	garlic cloves minced
½	chopped onion
½	tablespoon extra virgin olive oil
1	tablespoon basil
1	tablespoon oregano
16	ounce vermicelli, spaghetti or capelline

Heat olive oil in skillet and add garlic and onion and saute until tender. Add ground turkey and brown mashing with a fork to crumble as it cooks. Add pasta sauce and spices and serve over cooked pasta. *6 servings. ½ cup.*

You can add more spice according to your taste. By using turkey you are cutting the fat quite a lot. You will not cut the flavor!

Calories 374
Protein .... 21.2 G
Carbohydrates .... 61.7 G
Dietary Fiber .... 1.60 G
Fat-Total .... 4.39 G
Fat-Saturated .... 0.793 G
Sodium .... 258 Mg
Calories from fats 11%

Spaghetti a la Montanero

1	medium chopped onion (½ cup)
2	cloves garlic crushed
1	tablespoon extra virgin olive oil
4	strips "Mr. Turkey" bacon (julienned)
1	cup white wine (any kind will do)
2	16 ounce can whole tomatoes
⅛	teaspoon red pepper flakes

Saute onion, garlic, and Mr. Turkey in olive oil. Add wine and bring to a boil. Simmer and reduce until mixture thickens slightly. Chop tomatoes in bowl and add to bacon mixture. Add basil and red pepper flakes. You can add more red pepper to taste. (Be careful, it gets hotter as it cooks!) Simmer 20 minutes. Serve with spaghetti (thin) cooked al denté and mixed together. Can sprinkle Parmesan cheese on each serving. *6 servings. ½ cup.*

The original recipe was made with prosciutto ham. Go ahead for special occasions and use prosciutto or ¼ lb. very thinly sliced pancetta Your fat grams will be higher. This will probably be high in sodium. Also, prosciutto and pancetta can both be found in your Italian market, or ask your butcher for them at your local grocery store.

Calories	329
Protein	10.5 G
Carbohydrates	53.6 G
Dietary Fiber	2.05 G
Fat-Total	5.29 G
Fat-Saturated	0.700 G
Sodium	488 Mg
Calories from fats	14%

Capellini *a la Basil*

1	pound capellini pasta
4	garlic cloves minced
2	tablespoon olive oil extra virgin
1-2	tablespoons basil (Fresh would be better)

Saute garlic in olive oil, Cook, rinse and drain capellini, add to garlic and olive oil and coat until evenly covered. Add 1 more tablespoon olive oil and mix. Increase heat, add basil and continue coating until mixture is evenly covered and warm. You can add more basil for taste. Also you can add red pepper flakes, ⅛ teaspoon for more spice. Top with Parmesan cheese (I use Kraft fat-free or Weight Watchers).

This is a great side dish, or as a main course. Serve with a light salad and bread. This is very quick and easy to make. The more basil you use, the better the flavor will be. *Servings 8, 1 cup.*

```
Calories .............................. 253
Protein ............................ 7.49 G
Carbohydrates ................. 44.8 G
Dietary Fiber ................. 0.058 G
Fat-Total .......................... 4.33 G
Fat-Saturated ................ 0.458 G
Sodium ........................... 113 Mg
Calories from fats .............. 16%
```

Easy Risotto (Italian Rice)

2   cans chicken broth (Swanson makes a low sodium)
1   cup long grain rice (Arborio rice-Italian rice)
       saffron (a pinch, more if you like)
1   small can chopped mushrooms, drained (you can use
       ½ pound fresh instead)
       Kraft fat-free Parmesan cheese
       parsley flakes (sprinkle on before serving)

Heat broth in skillet. When broth comes to a boil, add rice, saffron, and mushrooms. Cover and cook until almost all liquid has cooked down. Cook on low simmer. Rice will be firm. Serve al denté (firm, never soft and sticky). *6 servings. ½ cup.*

The rice to use when making authentic risotto, is Arborio, however if you don't have it on hand, you can substitute with long grain rice. When making authentic Risotto the process of adding your liquid takes quite a lot of time. We have shortened this recipe to make it quick and easy for you!

This is an easy way to make a tasty rice! This is great with chicken broth with chicken cooked on the grill!

Calories 144
Protein .... 4.83 G
Carbohydrates .... 29.9 G
Dietary Fiber .... 1.05 G
Fat-Total .... 0.362 G
Fat-Saturated .... 0.077 G
Sodium .... 293 Mg
Calories from fats 2%

Elegant Skillet Rice with Herbs

1	tablespoon extra virgin olive oil
½	small chopped onion
2	16 ounce can chicken broth
1½	cups white rice long grain
1	teaspoon basil (You may use fresh. Double your amount if you do)
1	tablespoon parsley
1	teaspoon thyme
½	teaspoon red pepper flakes

Saute onion in olive oil. Add rice and gently cook until slightly brown on edges. Add chicken broth and bring to a boil. Cover and simmer until liquid is absorbed for approximately 20-25 minutes. Add all herbs and serve. *6 servings. ½ cup.*

This rice accompanies any meal! It is easy and elegant. For extra pizzaz add some frozen peas or any other veggie!

```
Calories ................................. 205
Protein ............................. 5.52 G
Carbohydrates ................. 39.1 G
Dietary Fiber .................. 0.914 G
Fat-Total ........................... 2.61 G
Fat-Saturated ................. 0.396 G
Sodium .............................. 323 G
Calories from fats ............... 12%
```

Easy Mexican Rice

1	cup long grain rice
1	14 ounce can whole tomatoes chopped or crushed
1	tablespoon extra virgin olive oil
1	can Campbell's beef consomme
1	chopped onion
1	tablespoon chili powder
	(I usually add more depending on taste)
	garlic salt- to taste

Brown rice and onion in olive oil until onions are clear. Add consomme, tomatoes, chili powder and dash of garlic salt. Stir and let boil for a minute, then transfer to glass casserole dish and bake covered for 45-60 minutes at 350°. *8 servings. ½-1 cup.*

This has a great spicy flavor! It's wonderful with any Mexican dish!

Calories 126
Protein .... 4.02 G
Carbohydrates .... 22.9 G
Dietary Fiber .... 1.12 G
Fat-Total .... 1.99 G
Fat-Saturated .... 0.292 G
Sodium .... 295 Mg
Calories from fats 14%

Tortellini Soup

6	cups chicken broth (use a low fat brand if possible)
1	19 oz. package beef tortellini
1	15 oz. can diced tomatoes
½	cup shredded fresh basil (it's important that you use fresh basil; it makes the recipe)
2-3	tablespoons Balsamic vinegar garnish with Parmesan cheese and fresh ground pepper

Bring chicken broth to a boil; add tortellini and cook for 5 minutes until tortellini floats to top. Remove from heat and add basil and tomatoes, then add vinegar and salt to taste. Serve in soup bowls.

This is an easy soup to make for a quick dinner! The whole family will love it! Serve with crusty bread. *4-6 servings. 1 cup each.*

If you cannot find beef tortellini in your freezer section, you may substitute it for cheese tortellini.

Calories 311
Protein .... 16 G
Carbohydrates .... 46 G
Dietary Fiber .... 2.57 G
Fat-Total .... 6.7 G
Fat-Saturated .... 3.921 G
Sodium .... 1049 Mg
Calories from fats 20%

Pasta Shrimp

1	(16 ounce) package penne pasta
¼	cup sun-dried tomatoes (not oil packed)
1	cup boiling water
1	package (16 ounce) Healthy Choice low-fat kielbasa
1	tablespoon olive oil
1	medium onion, cut into strips
1	large green pepper, cut into strips
1	large yellow pepper, cut into strips
4	tablespoons Italian seasoning
1	tablespoon chicken seasoning
1	tablespoon basil
2	tablespoons tarragon
2	pounds medium shrimp – no tails
2	cloves fresh garlic, minced
1	cup shredded Parmesan cheese
	fresh pepper to taste
	cayenne pepper to taste

Cook pasta according to package directions. Hydrate sun-dried tomatoes in boiling water and drain. Dice kielbasa into bite-size pieces. Cook in skillet over medium heat until slightly browned. Set aside. Heat olive oil in large pot. Sauté onion, peppers and spices over medium high heat until tender. Add shrimp, garlic and sun-dried tomatoes. Stir for 2 minutes. Add kielbasa, pasta and cheese. Stir to combine. Season with pepper to taste. *6 servings, ½ cup. Melissa Hamelink- Charlotte, North Carolina.*

To lower the fat, you may substitute your Parmesan cheese using a fat-free brand.

Calories	650
Protein	58 G
Carbohydrates	71 G
Dietary Fiber	2.620 G
Fat Total	12.356G
Fat-Saturated	4.66G
Sodium	1,375 MG
Calories from fat	17%

Powerful Proteins!

Chicken, Pork, Beef & Turkey

Oh so Easy!
Szechwan Chicken

4	skinless boned split chicken breasts, cut into 1½ inch cubes
5	tablespoons soy sauce (I use Kikkoman Lite)
1	teaspoon sugar
¼	cup water
⅛ to ¼	teaspoon cayenne pepper
3	tablespoon cornstarch
2	tablespoon extra virgin olive oil
3	garlic cloves minced
½-1	tablespoon white wine vinegar
1	bunch green onion sliced (1 inch diagonally including tops)

Place cornstarch in a paper bag. Add chicken pieces and shake to coat .Heat olive oil in skillet or wok. Add chicken and garlic and stir-fry until chicken is lightly browned. Add soy sauce, vinegar, sugar and water. Cover and cook 3-5 minutes. Add green onions and cayenne pepper. Heat until thoroughly blended. Serve over rice. If the chicken begins to stick, while you are sautéing, spray Pam lightly in pan . Also using a Teflon coated pan will help. This is so easy and elegant! *4 Servings. 1 breast.*

This is very quick and easy to prepare. It is also very spicy! You can cut down on the amount of cayenne. Remember you can always add more! You can't take the hot out!

Calories	198
Protein	19.5 G
Carbohydrates	7.73 G
Dietary Fiber	0.755 G
Fat-Total	8.71 G
Fat-Saturated	0.926 G
Sodium	754 Mg
Calories from fats	42%

Chicken Marsala

4	boneless skinless chicken breasts
1	tablespoon extra virgin olive oil
1	cup flour
½	pound fresh mushrooms, washed and sliced
½	medium onion or small onion chopped
½	bell pepper, sliced diagonally
1	teaspoon Italian seasoning
1	cup Marsala cooking wine
2	garlic cloves, minced or chopped fine

Flour chicken breasts and brown in oil on medium in skillet. If you find that you need more oil, spray PAM olive oil lightly on bottom of skillet. After browning breasts on both sides, remove from pan. Add mushrooms, onions, pepper and garlic to skillet. Sauté vegetables for 2 minutes, stirring constantly. Add marsala wine and cover and continue to cook on medium high to reduce liquid. Add Italian seasoning at this time. Add breasts to liquid and cover and simmer for 15 minutes. Serve with pasta of your choice! *4 Servings.*

I have found the easiest way to use fresh garlic cloves, is to peel them and mash them in a garlic press. Once you use one of these, you will love it! They can be found at most kitchen shops.

Calories 258
Protein .... 21.6 G
Carbohydrates .... 17.4 G
Dietary Fiber .... 2.09 G
Fat Total .... 5.68 G
Fat-Saturated.............. 0.518 G
Sodium .... 384 Mg
Calories of fats 20%

Cuban Chicken

4	boneless skinless chicken breasts (halves)
1	green pepper chopped
1	yellow onion chopped
1	tablespoon extra virgin olive oil
1	16 ounce can crushed tomatoes
2	cans 15 ounce size, Progresso black beans (drained)
1-2	tablespoon McCormick Cajun seasoning
2	tablespoon salsa (I use Pace Thick and Chunky medium spicy)
1	cup white rice, cooked

Brown chicken breasts in olive oil, along with your onion and pepper. Sprinkle generously with Cajun seasoning on both sides as the breasts are browning. Remove chicken and arrange in glass oblong casserole. Add tomatoes, beans and salsa to your green pepper and onion. Heat thoroughly and pour over chicken breasts. Cover and bake at 350° for 45 minutes to an hour. Prepare rice as chicken is cooking. Serve over rice! *4 Servings.*

This is one of those recipes I started experimenting with in the kitchen. Add more veggies if you like or different salsas or even a different seasoning! This has a great spicy flavor! Serve with lots of rice! The bean mixture is great over the rice!

```
Calories ................................. 467
Protein ............................ 34.8  G
Carbohydrates ................. 66.8  G
Dietary Fiber ................... 14.0  G
Fat-Total .......................... 7.58  G
Fat-Saturated ................ 0.592  G
Sodium ........................ 1157  Mg
Calories from fats ............... 14%
```

Moroccan Chicken

4	skinless boned chicken breasts
¼	cup all purpose flour
½	teaspoon ground cumin
¼	teaspoon pepper
1	tablespoon olive oil
2	carrots chopped in chunks
1	large red onion, sliced
1	medium zucchini, cut into chucks
1	(28 oz) can peeled tomatoes (chopped)
1	large garlic clove (minced)
1	teaspoon dried oregano
1	tablespoon parsley (you can use fresh or dry)

On wax paper, stir flour, cumin and pepper; dredge chicken in mixture. In large skillet, coated with olive oil, add chicken and cook on medium heat until evenly browned on both sides. Remove and set aside. Respray skillet and add all of your vegetables and sauté just until softened. Add chicken and tomatoes and Oregano. Simmer until chicken is cooked. This dish is great served with cous cous! Remember: cous cous is great cooked in chicken broth instead of water! Do not overcook your zucchini! You want it to still have a crunch! *4 Servings. 1 Chicken breast.*

Calories	232
Protein	23.1 G
Carbohydrates	23.6 G
Dietary-Fiber	4.74 G
Fat-Total	6.08 G
Fat-Saturated	0.586 G
Sodium	338 Mg
Calories from fats	23%

Chicken Piccata

4	skinless boneless chicken breasts, lightly breaded with flour
2	tablespoon olive oil (extra virgin light)
3	garlic cloves minced or crushed
1	teaspoon marjoram
1	lemon
1½	cups white wine or white cooking wine (found in the salad dressing section, usually)
½	cup flour (use as much as needed)

Brown chicken breasts in olive oil. Remove breasts from pan. Add wine and garlic and bring to a boil. Reduce wine, stirring until liquid is reduced to half. Squeeze ½ lemon into sauce and simmer. Add chicken to mixture; Add marjoram, pepper to taste. Simmer for 10 minutes. Serve with remainder of lemon sliced thin as a garnish on the side. *4 Servings. 1 breast.*

If your chicken breasts are too thick, you can pound them with a meat tenderizer, on both sides, until they are thin enough. This makes your meat tender. This recipe is usually made with veal, instead of chicken, we cut the fat down by making it with chicken. Veal Piccata is served in elegant Italian restaurants, we think our's is almost as good, using chicken!

```
Calories ............................ 238  G
Protein ............................ 19.2  G
Carbohydrates ................. 1.88  G
Dietary Fiber ................. 0.077  G
Fat-Total .......................... 8.67  G
Fat- Saturated .............. 0.916  G
Sodium ....................... 0.932  Mg
Calories from fats ............... 32%
```

Grilled Chicken Breasts

4-6	chicken breasts
2	large cloves garlic, mashed or minced
½	cup soy sauce (2 use Kikkoman Lite)
½-¾	cup packed brown sugar

Trim any excess fat from breasts. Put in glass casserole dish. Add soy sauce, garlic and brown sugar. Stir until mixture is evenly distributed. You can marinate this for as long as you want or if you are in a hurry, just a few minutes to an hour. Grill on the Bar B Que pit 8-10 minutes per side. *4-6 Servings. 1 breast.*

This is a great marinade for chicken. Stir-fry chicken is great made with this marinade. Serve this with colorful veggies and rice and you've got an easy elegant meal!

Calories	219
Protein	19.0 G
Carbohydrates	27.0 G
Dietary Fiber	0.025 G
Fat-Total	1.90 G
Fat-Saturated	0.001 G
Sodium	1210 Mg
Calories from fats	8%

Black Bean and Lime Chicken

3-4	boneless chicken breasts
1-2	pounds tomatoes (sliced) may peel if prefer
1	tablespoon olive oil virgin extra light
1	green onion chopped including top
2-3	cloves of garlic minced
1	teaspoon cumin
1	tablespoon fresh lime juice or juice 1 lime
1	can Progresso black beans (15 ounce) (drain)
1	tablespoon cilantro

Brown chicken breasts in olive oil and garlic. Season chicken with cumin as it is browning. Add green onion, tomatoes, lime juice, beans and rest of spices. Heat thoroughly. Transfer to glass casserole dish and bake 45 minutes, covered at 350°. Serve with rice. *4 servings. 1 breast.*

Calories 300
Protein .... 36.3 G
Carbohydrates .... 19.1 G
Dietary Fiber .... 7 G
Fat Total .... 8.4 G
Fat Saturated .... 1.8 G
Sodium .... 3.7 Mg
Calories from fat 25%

Chicken and Spinach Enchiladas

1	package "Pinata" brand flour tortillas (12.5 ounce size)
1½	pound boneless skinless chicken breasts
1	10 ounce package chopped frozen spinach
⅓	cup chopped onion
1	teaspoon olive oil (extra virgin light)
¼	cup skim milk
1	4-ounce can chopped green chilies
1	8 ounce carton non fat plain yogurt
1	cup fat-free Healthy Choice Cheddar cheese
1	can Healthy Request cream of chicken soup

Boil chicken breasts and dice. Cook spinach (I microwave it right in the box). Squeeze spinach, and reserve ½ cup of juice. Sauté onion in olive oil. Stir in chicken and spinach. Set aside. Combine soup, spinach broth, skim milk, green chilies, yogurt and ½ Cheddar cheese in bowl. Add ½ of the sauce to your chicken mixture. Begin filling each tortilla with chicken mixture and roll, keeping seam side down. Be sure to spray pan with a small amount of olive oil spray. Pour remaining sauce over top of tortillas. Sprinkle remaining cheddar cheese on top. Bake at 350° for 25 minutes. *10 enchiladas. 2 per servings. Suzy Hamelink- Charlotte, North Carolina.*

These enchiladas have a lot of flavor! You won't miss any of the fat in this recipe! These take a little bit of time to prepare, but are well worth the effort! These are great served with the Mexican rice recipe.

Calories	448
Protein	42.0 G
Carbohydrates	56.7 G
Dietary Fiber	4.34 G
Fat-Total	7.54 G
Fat-Saturated	0.850 G
Sodium	1062 Mg
Calories from fats	15%

Chicken or Turkey Parmesan

6	turkey cutlets, or you may use boneless skinless chicken breasts (if thick, pound into thin scallop size)
½	cup Progresso Italian bread crumbs
½	cup Kraft fat-free Parmesan cheese
½	teaspoon paprika
8	ounce fat-free Mozzarella cheese
1	8 ounce can tomato sauce
	garlic salt lightly to taste
1	teaspoon oregano
2	egg whites lightly beaten
	PAM (use several sprays, you might have to respray your pan if it is too dry)

Mix Parmesan cheese and bread crumbs together. Mix egg whites in separate bowl. Dip chicken or turkey cutlets in egg and then crumbs. Brown in pan sprayed with PAM. Remove and put in glass 9 x 9 oblong casserole dish. Lay cheese over each piece of meat. Mix garlic, oregano and tomato sauce together and pour over meat. Bake at 350° for 50 minutes. Uncover last 5 minutes. *6 servings. 1 cutlet.*

This makes a great dinner! Your guests will think you are serving them Veal Parmesiana! Since we are substituting our cheeses, you might want to use more oregano for flavoring. As a quick sauce alternative, buy your favorite low-fat spaghetti sauce and pour over instead of mixing your own. Healthy Choice makes a good one or Ragu "light basil." Find one that tastes good, and also is low-fat at the same time. This is one of those easy recipes that people will think you spent a lot of time in the kitchen over!

Calories	628
Protein	113 G
Carbohydrates	18.3 G
Dietary Fiber	0.977 G
Fat-Total	6.69 G
Fat-Saturated	0.017 G
Sodium	2675 Mg
Calories from fats	7%

Grilled Turkey Breast Steaks

4	turkey breast steaks (I use Honeysuckle White found in the freezer section)
½	teaspoon garlic salt
½	teaspoon McCormick Cajun seasoning
1	teaspoon cilantro
	(approx. ¼ pound each)

Sprinkle each turkey breast with each of the spices. Broil in oven on second rack until cooked. 8-10 minutes. Be sure not to over cook. *4 servings. 1 turkey breast.*

We analyzed this 2 ways for you, using garlic powder versus garlic salt! Look at your sodium difference.

Using garlic salt
Calories 486
Protein .... 97.2 G
Carbohydrates .... 0.002 G
Dietary Fiber .... 0.001 G
Fat-Total .... 6.08 G
Fat-Saturated .... 0 G
Sodium .... 2118 G
Calories from fats 11%

Using garlic powder
Calories 486
Protein .... 97.3 G
Carbohydrates .... 0.257 G
Dietary Fiber .... 0.007 G
Fat-Total .... 6.08 G
Fat-Saturated .... 0.001 G
Sodium .... 1993 Mg
Calories from fats 11%

Easy Chicken and Rice

4-6	skinless boneless chicken breasts, rinsed and patted dry
1	tablespoon extra virgin olive oil light
1	cup flour
1	tablespoon paprika- pepper to taste
1	can Healthy Request cream of chicken soup
¾	cup white wine (can use any kind you might have on hand or white cooking wine)

Mix flour and paprika together on plate. Heat olive oil in medium skillet. Dip breasts in flour and coat both sides. Brown breasts in olive oil. Remove from skillet and place in 9 x 12 glass casserole dish. Spoon cream of chicken soup over breasts. Pour wine over. Cover and bake 350 degrees for 45 minutes to an hour. Make a double serving of white rice and serve over rice. The gravy is great on the rice! *Serving size: 1 breast, 1 person.*

Tip: Since we are using less olive oil for browning, use a Teflon coated skillet. This will help prevent sticking. You might also need to spray your skillet with Pam.

My family loves this recipe! It is quick and easy and makes great gravy over rice! This makes an easy and quick dinner, all you need is a salad or your favorite veggie!

Calories 231
Protein .... 21.3 G
Carbohydrates .... 14.7 G
Dietary Fiber .... 0.571 G
Fat-Total .... 6.81 G
Fat-Saturated .... .11 G
Sodium .... 303 Mg
Calories from fats 1%

Spicy Chicken Soup

4	cups canned low-sodium chicken broth (there are several on the market, choose your favorite)
1	cup chopped onion
1	cup chopped red pepper
1	cup chopped green pepper
1	cup chopped fresh tomato (1)
1	teaspoon oregano
1	4.5 ounce can chopped green chilies (this is the small size)
2	teaspoon chili powder
2	teaspoon cumin
	pepper to taste
1	bay leaf
3	skinned boned chicken breast halves, cooked and diced
1-2	ounce Healthy Choice fat-free Mozzarella shredded cheese or Kraft ⅓ less-fat shredded cheese of your choice

Combine first 10 ingredients in a stew pot. Stir well and bring to a boil. Cover, and reduce heat, and simmer for 35 minutes. Remove bay leaf and add cooked, diced chicken and continue to cook until thoroughly heated. Serve soup in bowls with shredded cheese on top. You can serve any low-fat tortilla chips with this. Almost all of the low-fat brands have only 1 gram of fat per 13 chips. Some are even less fat. Enjoy! *4 servings. 1 cup.*

Remember: You can experiment with these flavors by adding or omitting the seasonings of your choice.

This soup has all the veggies that are good for you in it!

Calories 228
Protein .... 36.3 G
Carbohydrates .... 17.5 G
Dietary Fiber .... 3.09 G
Fat-Total .... 2.04 G
Fat-Saturated .... 0.112 G
Sodium .... 879 Mg
Calories from fats 8%

Stir Fry
Chicken Fajitas

4	skinless boned chicken breasts, cut in strips
1	tablespoon extra virgin olive oil
1	green pepper cut in strips
1	red pepper cut in strips
1	small onion chopped
1-1½	tablespoon Cajun seasoning
1	can green chilies, chopped (use the small can)
2	tablespoon picante sauce mild or salsa of your choice
2	tablespoon Healthy Choice Cheddar cheese or if you prefer Cheddar ⅓ less-fat by Kraft
1	package flour tortillas
1	tablespoon Land O' Lakes no-fat sour cream shredded lettuce
2	tomatoes chopped

Sauté chicken strips in olive oil. Sprinkle chicken with Cajun seasoning as you are sautéing . Set aside. Cook vegetables separately until tender, but still crisp. You may use PAM or a very small amount of olive oil. Heat tortillas per package directions and then fill tortillas with meat mixture and vegetables. Add your own sour cream, cheese, tomatoes, etc. to your taste. *5 servings (2 tortillas per serving).*

My Easy Mexican rice is great with this! This is another recipe that you can be creative with! You know which veggies your family love, and the ones they don't, so make this your way, using your favorites!

Calories 434
Protein .... 32.6 G
Carbohydrates .... 60.2 G
Dietary Fiber .... 4.04 G
Fat-Total .... 7.50 G
Fat-Saturated .... 0.406 G
Sodium .... 1550 Mg
Calories from fats 15%

Chicken Shish-K-Bobs

4	chicken breasts boned and skinned
¼	cup soy sauce
¼	cup diet Russian dressing or Catalina (fat-free)
2	tablespoon lemon juice
3	cloves garlic crushed
¼	teaspoon ginger
1	large green pepper cut into chunks
1	onion, cut into chunks
3	zucchini, cut into ¾-inch pieces
1	pint cherry tomatoes
1	pint fresh mushrooms (whole)

Mix all ingredients and marinate meat in for 2 hours. Fill skewers with meat and vegetables. Cook 6 inches over medium hot coals on skewers, 15-20 minutes basting with marinade. If you are using wooden skewers please be sure to soak them in water before you add your ingredients, this keeps them from burning. Also, space your ingredients ¼-inch apart on skewer, this will help cook your ingredients evenly. This is great served with rice. *6-8 servings. Gretchen Heinz- Springfield, Missouri.*

This served with rice makes a great dinner for company anytime.

Calories 188
Protein .... 22.0 G
Carbohydrates .... 18.8 G
Dietary Fiber .... 3.53 G
Fat-Total .... 2.54 G
Fat-Saturated .... 0.096 G
Sodium .... 790 Mg
Calories from fats 12%

Spicy Pork Chop Casserole

4	lean butterfly loin chops (4 ounces each)
1	can Campbell's soup (beef consommé)
1	cup white rice
1	small onion chopped
1-2	tablespoon chili powder
1	16 ounce can crushed tomatoes (may use whole)
	PAM olive oil spray
	garlic salt to taste

Brown pork chops in skillet. Transfer to a 9 x 12 oblong glass casserole. Spray PAM in skillet and add onion and rice, and brown. Add tomatoes, consommé and chili powder. Bring to a boil and pour over pork chops Cover and bake 45-60 minutes at 350°. *4 servings. 1 pork chop.*

This recipe came from Pasadena, California and has been in my family for many years! This makes a complete meal in one dish! You can add more or less chili powder depending on your taste.

Calories	389
Protein	32.7 G
Carbohydrates	48.0 G
Dietary Fiber	3.36 G
Fat-Total	7.63 G
Fat-Saturated	2.58 G
Sodium	675 Mg
Calories from fats	18%

Teriyaki Pork Tenderloin

1	16 ounce pork tenderloin (these are in the meat department sometimes there are 2 per package)
¾	cup Kikkoman Lite soy sauce
2-3	garlic cloves minced
½	cup packed brown sugar

Marinate pork tenderloin in mixture of soy sauce, brown sugar and garlic. If you have time, marinate for several hours. If not, any length of time is fine. Broil in oven or cook or grill. Slice in ¼ inch slices. *(3-5) 4 ounce servings.*

You can always add more brown sugar to your marinade for a sweeter taste. This is an easy meat to prepare. Serve with your favorite veggies and salad and you'll have a complete meal. Pork is a tasty meat to prepare, and there are a million ways to marinate it! Since our marinade basically only has soy sauce and brown sugar in it, we are not adding any fat to the meat, and pork is not high in fat!

Calories 275
Protein .... 24.0 G
Carbohydrates .... 27.2 G
Dietary Fiber .... 0.037 G
Fat-Total .... 3.99 G
Fat-Saturated .... 1.49 G
Sodium .... 1864 Mg
Calories from fats 12%

Gingered Pork

2-3	pork tenderloins
1	cup soy sauce
¼	cup sugar
1	small; minced onion
1-2	garlic cloves minced
1	tablespoon Worcestershire sauce
1	teaspoon grated ginger to taste
4	tablespoons sesame seeds

Place tenderloins in glass baking dish. Spray bottom of pan with olive oil spray. Sprinkle with sesame seeds. Pour marinade over and marinate for 3 hours or more and refrigerate. Drain and bake 375° for 1 hour. Slice and serve on small rye bread or dollar buns. If you would like to use your leftover marinade as a sauce, please boil before using. *6-8 servings, depending on size and weight of pork tenderloin. 1 piece. Doris Stinnett. St. Louis, Missouri*

My sister-in-law always makes this recipe for company. It's great with mostaciolli as a side dish! It's great served on small sandwich buns or even better, as a main course with a veggie and a salad. We have taken some of the fat out by omitting the butter during baking.

Calories 129
Protein .... 17.8 G
Carbohydrates .... 5 G
Dietary Fiber .... .3 G
Fat-Total .... 3.8 G
Fat-Saturated .... 1.1 G
Sodium .... 808 Mg
Calories from fats 34%

Gingered Pork
with Snow Peas

1-1½	pounds pork loin cut in 1 inch pieces
¾	cup lite soy sauce
1	tablespoon ginger
1	tablespoon extra virgin olive oil
2	cup Healthy Choice or low sodium chicken broth
½	cup sherry
	salt and pepper
1	package Birds Eye frozen snow peas
1	tablespoon cornstarch dissolved in water

Marinate the pork in mixture of soy sauce and ginger for a few hours or 1-2 if short on time. Remove and brown in olive oil. Bake at 350° in chicken broth and sherry for 1 hour or until tender. Thicken mixture with cornstarch. Add frozen snow peas to hot meat and gravy and serve with rice. If you prefer, you can quickly blanch your snow peas before adding them. *6 servings.*

This is a great recipe for company! Serve over rice and wait for all the compliments!

Calories 285
Protein .... 30.0 G
Carbohydrates .... 5.38 G
Dietary Fiber .... 0.067 G
Fat-Total .... 6.95 G
Fat-Saturated .... 2.06 G
Sodium .... 1424 Mg
Calories from fats 22%

Sicilian Pork Chops

4	butterfly pork loin chops pounded and lightly breaded with flour
1	tablespoon extra virgin olive oil (I try to find light)
1	cup Marsala wine or Marsala cooking wine
½	tablespoon marjoram
1	16 ounce can crushed tomatoes
1	tablespoon oregano
¼	teaspoon red pepper flakes

Trim any fat from chops. Brown breaded chops in olive oil. Cover and simmer gently. Remove from skillet and set aside. Add wine and simmer slowly to reduce liquid. Add tomatoes and spices. Add pork chops back to pan with sauce, cover and simmer gently for 10 minutes. Serve with pasta. Can use sauce over it for a side dish of pasta. *4 servings. 1 pork chop. Matt Stinnett-Springfield, Missouri*

This has a great flavor, and my husband and teenage son experimented with this recipe together.

Calories 388
Protein .... 37.4 G
Carbohydrates. .... 9.70 G
Dietary Fiber .... 1.42 G
Fat-Total .... 15.7 G
Fat-Saturated .... 4.62 G
Sodium .... 653 Mg
Calories from fats 36%

Pork Tenderloin

1-2   pound pork tenderloin
1   ounce bottle Hidden Valley ranch fat-free Italian Parmesan dressing

Marinate pork in salad dressing for as long as possible. Several hours. Cook on grill. *4 servings.*

Pork tenderloins are great marinated in just about any salad dressing. Be sure to check for fat grams and sodium. It is usually high in bottled dressings.

Calories 314
Protein .... 47.7 G
Carbohydrates .... 7.09 G
Dietary Fiber .... 0 G
Fat-Total .... 7.96 G
Fat-Saturated .... 2.98 G
Sodium .... 535 Mg
Calories from fats 23%

Lite Bar-B-Que Beef

1-2½   lb. eye of round or arm roast
1   cup water
1   teaspoon white vinegar
1   teaspoon lemon juice
1   small onion chopped fine
1   teaspoon salt
1   teaspoon I Can't Believe its Not Butter- light margarine
1   teaspoon salt (optional)
¼   teaspoon black pepper
¼   teaspoon cayenne
1   tablespoon prepared mustard
1½ -2 cups Bar B Que sauce (I use a gourmet sauce that is sweet and spicy)

Combine all ingredients in a covered pot. Simmer roast for 4-5 hours or until meat crumbles. Drain liquid and shred meat with a fork and add Bar B Que sauce. Serve on warm buns. *10-½ cup servings. Sue Throckmorton-Wildwood, Missouri*

I have used a lean cut of beef to lower the fat content. Add your favorite flavor of Bar B Que sauce! This is a great dish to have on hand for company. This serves a lot of people and is so easy to fix. My sister-in-law, Sue, makes this for her large family. This is one of those meals to fix when you know that you are going to have a lot of hungry teenagers or men! Sue butters the buns and sprinkles them with garlic salt and then broils them. This makes them extra rich, and does add some fat, so remember that when buttering the buns!

Calories 206
Protein .... 26.9 G
Carbohydrates. .... 5.21 G
Dietary Fiber .... 0.522 G
Fat-Total .... 8.00 G
Fat-Saturated .... 2.58 G
Sodium .... 814 Mg
Calories from fats 36%

Flank Steak
"A la Bar B Que"

1 -2   pound lean flank steak
1   16 ounce bottle of your favorite Bar B Que sauce (I try to use one that has a smoky or sweet flavor)

Trim any visible fat from flank steak. Marinate in glass casserole dish in 8 ounces of Bar B Que sauce. The longer, the better, but even if you can only marinate this for an hour it will still be great! Grill on the pit until rare. Cut into diagonal strips on the bias and serve. *4 servings.*

This has a wonderful flavor! Great for company and so easy! This is one of those quick meats to throw on the pit when you invite someone for a spur of the moment dinner. Add a salad, potato of your choice, and you have a quick, easy meal!

Make sure you serve this medium rare. It is very juicy and tender this way. If it's over cooked, it will be dry.

Calories 338
Protein .... 40.3 G
Carbohydrates .... 7.50 G
Dietary Fiber. .... 0.469 G
Fat-Total .... 16.0 G
Fat-Saturated .... 6.05 G
Sodium .... 749 Mg
Calories from fats 43%

Asian Marinated Flank Steak

1-1½	pound flank steak
½	cup brown sugar
⅓	cup dark sesame oil
½	cup soy sauce
⅓	cup dry red wine
3	cloves fresh garlic, minced
2	tablespoons fresh gingerroot, minced

Combine all ingredients and place in plastic bag. Marinate in refrigerator at least 6 hours or overnight. Remove steak from marinade-discard marinade. Grill to desired degree of doneness. Slice diagonally across grain. This is best when sliced very thin on the bias. It is also more tender if served medium rare. This is a great cut of meat to keep on hand for grilling. A great company dish! *4 servings. Melissa Hamelink-Charlotte, North Carolina.*

The fat content came out very high; however, remember that you are not using the marinade. We evaluated just the meat and the actual fat grams are only 12.6G per serving.

Calories 556
Protein .... 37.7 G
Carbohydrates .... 19.705 G
Dietary Fiber .... 189 G
Fat Total .... 33 G
Fat-Saturated 8.472G
Sodium .... 1188 G
Calories from fat 55%

98

Scrumptious Seafood!

Garlic Shrimp

24	large shrimp cleaned and deveined
1	tablespoon extra virgin olive oil
6	crushed garlic cloves
1	cup white wine (any brand will do or a cooking wine)
½	cup bread crumbs (not seasoned)
1	tablespoon parsley
	lemon slice for garnish

Saute garlic in olive oil in skillet. After it's lightly browned, add your shrimp stirring, as they cook on medium heat. Add wine and continue to cook as liquid reduces. After wine has reduced to ½ the liquid, add your bread crumbs, continuing to stir until shrimp is lightly coated. Add parsley to top. Serve with white rice. *4 servings. 6 shrimp.*

You can use jumbo shrimp if you prefer. This is a great dish for entertaining! You can be preparing this, as your guests watch!

Calories 171
Protein .... 10.7 G
Carbohydrates .... 11.4 G
Dietary Fiber .... 0.631 G
Fat-Total .... 4.77 G
Fat-Saturated .... 0.789 G
Sodium .... 159 G
Calories from fats 25%

Linguine Shrimp Dijongé

1½	pound fresh shrimp (shelled and deveined) (I prefer large sized shrimp)
¼	cup extra virgin olive oil
½	chopped yellow onion
2	garlic cloves minced
2	teaspoon Cajun seasoning (I use McCormick)
¼	cup white wine
1	tablespoon basil
1	16 ounce can crushed tomatoes
1	16 ounce package linguini
	tabasco sauce to taste

Saute garlic, onion and shrimp in olive oil until onions are clear. Add 1 teaspoon Cajun seasoning. Add wine and simmer 2 minutes. Add tomatoes, basil, Tabasco and 1 teaspoon Cajun seasoning and simmer for 15 minutes. Serve over linguini. *4 servings. ½ cup sauce. 1 cup pasta.*

If you feel you have made too much pasta and you want more of a sauce, you can only use ¾ pound instead. This is another one of those recipes you can cook in front of your quests as they watch! They'll love it!

Calories 561
Protein .... 14.8 G
Carbohydrates .... 87.2 G
Dietary Fiber .... 1.74 G
Fat-Total .... 15.8 G
Fat-Saturated .... 1.87 G
Sodium .... 706 Mg
Calories from fats 26%

Easy Shrimp Creole

1	pound shrimp (cooked and peeled)
1	tablespoon extra virgin olive oil
1	16 ounce can stewed tomatoes
½	can tomato soup
½	can tomato sauce
2	tablespoon Worcestershire sauce
½	cup minced onion
½	cup minced celery
½	cup minced green pepper
1	teaspoon sugar
½	teaspoon vinegar
	creole seasoning to taste

Cook shrimp and peel, or purchase already cooked and peeled. Saute onion, celery and green pepper in olive oil. Add tomatoes, soup and tomato sauce. Add sugar, vinegar and Worcestershire sauce and simmer until mixture thickens. Simmer for 1 hour or longer, and add cooked shrimp right before serving to heat. Add creole seasoning to taste. Serve over white rice. *4 servings. Doris Stinnett- St. Louis, Missouri*

```
Calories ................................. 177
Protein ............................. 21.5 G
Carbohydrates ................. 11.7 G
Dietary Fiber .................... 1.50 G
Fat-Total ........................... 5.45 G
Fat-Saturated ................. 0.630 G
Sodium ........................... 713 Mg
Calories from fats .............. 27%
```

Shrimp Diablo

1	pound shrimp cooked and deveined
1	tablespoon olive oil (extra light)
3	garlic cloves crushed
½	onion chopped
½	teaspoon red pepper flakes
½	teaspoon oregano
3	tablespoon fresh basil (chopped fine) or you may use dry which would be ½ the amount
1	16 ounce can crushed tomatoes
½	cup white wine or white cooking wine (any brand will do)
1	pound vermicelli, linguini or pasta of your choice salt and pepper to taste (optional)

Saute garlic and onion in olive oil. Add wine and simmer on low to reduce liquid. Add remaining ingredients and simmer 30 minutes. Serve over pasta or you may mix together. Enjoy!
6 servings (½ - ¾ cup each) sauce (1 cup pasta).

Calories 426
Protein 26g
Carbohydrates 61g
Dietary Fiber 1.3g
Fat Total 4.5g
Fat Saturated 0.5g
Sodium 333mg
Calories from fats 10.4%

Blackened Cajun Catfish

4   fresh catfish fillets
       paprika
1   tablespoon cajun seasoning (found in spice section)
       PAM olive oil spray
       cast iron skillet

Spray skillet with olive oil spray. Heat skillet on high. Turn broiler on in oven. Lightly season catfish fillets with paprika and Cajun seasoning evenly on both sides. After skillet is hot, add fillets and sear. Place cast iron skillet and fillets in broiler. Broil for 8 minutes on each side in skillet and serve immediately! *4 servings. 1 fillet per person.*

This is a quick and easy fish recipe! Great for last minute dinners!

```
Calories ................................. 137
Protein .............................. 20.9 G
Carbohydrates ............... 0.962 G
Dietary Fiber .................. 0.360 G
Fat-Total ........................... 5.05 G
Fat-Saturated ................... 1.13 G
Sodium ........................... 852 Mg
Calories from fats ............... 34%
```

Maré Monté

1	6.5 ounce can minced clams
½	pound sea scallops
½	pound shrimp peeled and deveined
1	clove garlic minced
6	sliced mushrooms (fresh)
1	chopped Roma tomato (½ cup)
1	cup white wine or cooking wine
1	tablespoon extra virgin olive oil
1-2	teaspoons basil
1	pound linguini (cooked al denté)

Saute garlic in olive oil. Add clams, including juice and rest of seafood, cooking on medium heat. Add wine and mushrooms, and continue to simmer for 20 minutes then add tomatoes. Add basil and pepper 5 minutes before serving. Combine sauce into linguine cooked al denté. Sprinkle parsley on top. Parmesan cheese to taste. *4 servings. ½ cup.*

This seafood pasta will get rave reviews from your company! Add some sourdough bread, a salad and you can serve this dish to your most discriminating guests! Versions of this seafood pasta are served in every great Italian restaurant that I have ever been to. Many times the seafood combination is changed according to what is available, but no matter which seafood is used, it always tastes great! This will be a winner with your guests!

Calories 664
Protein .... 42.1 G
Carbohydrates .... 95.3 G
Dietary Fiber .... 1.42 G
Fat-Total .... 7.17 G
Fat-Saturated .... 0.591 G
Sodium .... 590 Mg
Calories from fats 10%

Lime Marinated Grilled Salmon

2	pounds salmon fillets cut into 4-5 ounce portions (I do not recommend using the steaks, they have too many bones)
⅓	cup freshly squeezed lime juice
2	cups coarsely chopped onion
½-1	teaspoon coarsely chopped garlic
2	large jalapeños, minced
1	bunch fresh cilantro, coarsely chopped
1	teaspoon salt

Combine marinade ingredients in the work bowl of a food processor and pulse for 30 seconds. Taste and adjust seasonings.

Pour half of the marinade over the bottom of a glass or stainless steel baking dish. Place the fillets on the marinade, and pour the remaining marinade to cover the fillets. Marinate for at least 1 hour at room temperature, or refrigerate overnight. Wipe the marinade form the salmon, sprinkle the fish with salt and pepper to taste, and grill the salmon to desired doneness. This is served at the school with a ginger-Lime Butter and a Corn, Tomato and Black Bean Salsa. We omitted the Ginger-lime Butter, however any Black Bean Salsa is great served on the side.

While vacationing in Santa Fe, New Mexico, my family and I visited the Santa Fe School of Cooking shop and purchased their book. The salmon recipe is so good that I wanted to add it to the book. Susan Curtis who is the owner of the school was gracious enough to give me permission to use their recipe for my book. If you are ever in the Santa Fe area, please make sure you visit. They offer classes on many aspects of Southwestern cuisine, from traditional to contemporary. You will be glad that you did. *6-8 servings. 1 fillet each.*

Calories 201
Protein .... 31 G
Carbohydrates .... 6.265 G
Dietary Fiber .... 1.155 G
Fat Total .... 5 G
Fat Saturated .... 862 G
Sodium .... 490 Mg
Calories from fats 24%

Honey and Orange Spice Salmon

4	salmon fillets, cut into 4-5 ounce portions
1	stick unsalted butter
⅓	cup honey
⅓	cup packed brown sugar
2	tablespoons fresh squeezed orange juice from 1 orange
1	teaspoon liquid smoke
1	pinch cayenne pepper (adjust to taste; this continues to get hotter as it cooks)

Combine butter, honey, brown sugar, orange juice, cayenne, and liquid smoke in a saucepan. Heat on medium until smooth and creamy. Remove from heat, and cool to room temperature. Arrange salmon pieces in a small baking dish so that they are touching. Pour marinade over the salmon and marinate for 45 minutes turning once. Drain off marinade and discard. Grill salmon over red hot coals or broil skin side up on a broiler rack. Turn over and continue to broil other side. Broil 5-7 minutes on each side. Make sure your salmon has a flaky texture. You will have a caramelized texture on top. Do not burn. This is similar to a recipe served at the Citizen Kane restaurant in St. Louis. After trying it several times we think that it tastes almost as good! *4 servings. 1 fillet each.*

The butter in this recipe raises your fat grams quite a bit, however, using margarine would compromise the taste, so we decided to use butter. My son likes to use the sauce to spoon over the cooked salmon. If you do use the sauce, reserve some after you have heated it and before you use as a marinade. Do not use the marinade sauce before it has been thoroughly heated.

Calories	479
Protein	29 G
Carbohydrates	35.224 G
Dietary Fiber	.071 G
Fat Total	28 G
Fat Saturated	15.781 G
Sodium	65 Mg
Calories from fats	53 %

Southwest Missouri Smoked Trout

1-2	pound fresh trout (these are available at most seafood grocery store departments if you haven't had time for your own catch)
¼	cup liquid smoke
¼	cup balsamic vinegar
1	cup hickory chips (soaked in water 30 minutes)
1	red onion, chopped
1	small jar capers (found in olive & pickle section of your grocery store)
	toasted bread (any kind) cut into triangle pieces (Sourdough is good or if you are in a hurry, melba toast can be substituted. *You can figure on 2-3 per person. 8-10 servings for an appetizer, 2 for an entrée.*)

Marinate trout in liquid smoke and balsamic vinegar in a covered dish for 2-4 hours. Remove and smoke. Place coals on outside of grill and add your moist hickory chips on top of coals. Place trout on the middle of the grill and cover for 1 hour. Refrigerate trout after grilling to make sure it is good and chilled for 3 hours before serving. Serve with capers, red onion and toast on the side as an appetizer. My husband and son are both avid fly fishermen. After fishing one of Missouri's finest streams, my husband usually brings home at least 1 trout to smoke. He created this recipe and we frequently serve this as an appetizer for our dinner guests. It also makes a light supper served with a rice dish and salad. Enjoy!

Calories 271
Protein .... 23 G
Carbohydrates .... 27 G
Dietary Fiber .... 14 G
Fat Total .... 6.714 G
Fat Saturated .... 1.818 G
Sodium .... 428 Mg
Calories from fats 22%

Decadent Desserts!

Watermelon Sorbet

½   small watermelon seeded and cut into 1 inch chunks
3   tablespoon confectioners sugar
1   tablespoon lemon juice
¼   teaspoon salt

Early in day or up to 1 month ahead blend 1 cup watermelon chunks with sugar, lemon juice and salt until smooth in blender. Add remaining melon and blend a few seconds until smooth. Pour into 9 x 9 baking pan and freeze until partially frozen. After 1½ hours, spoon mixture into chilled bowl and mix on medium speed until fluffy, but still frozen. Return mixture to baking pan cover and refreeze until firm about 1½ hours.

To serve:
Let ice stand at room temperature about 10 minutes to soften slightly. Then scrape across surface with spoon to create snow flake icy texture. Spoon into dessert dishes. This is pretty, garnished with fresh mint.

This takes a little bit of time to make, but it is well worth the effort! This can be made ahead and kept in the freezer until needed. It is a very tasty sorbet! *6 servings. ½ cup.*

Calories 250
Protein .... 3 G
Carbohydrates .... 60 G
Dietary Fiber .... 2.4 G
Fat Total 0
Fat Saturated 0
Sodium .... 590 Mg
Calories from fats 0%

Forgotten Pudding

5   egg whites
½   teaspoon cream of tartar
¼   teaspoon salt
1 ½   cups sugar, less 2 tablespoon
1   teaspoon vanilla
1   pint whipped topping (Cool Whip)
        fresh fruit of our choice

Beat egg whites until foamy, add cream of tartar and salt. Continue beating and add sugar gradually. Add vanilla when meringue is stiff. Spread mixture in greased 9 x 12 glass pan. Preheat 425° oven, put meringue in and turn off oven, overnite. Open the next day and you will have a beautiful stiff meringue. Spread with whipped topping. Cut into squares and serve your favorite fruit on top. This makes a beautiful dessert! Strawberries, blueberries or peaches are especially great on top. *9 servings. Eileen Stahlhut- Town and Country, Missouri.*

Make sure you don't make this on a rainy day! Your guests will all love this elegant dessert! Our close family friend was kind enough to give this recipe to my family and we've enjoyed it for many years!

Calories 209
Protein .... 2 G
Carbohydrates .... 40 G
Dietary Fiber 0
Fat Total .... 4.2 G
Fat Saturated .... 4.2 G
Sodium .... 95 Mg
Calories from fats 38%

Soy Smoothie

1   cup soy milk (I try to find a low-fat brand choose, either plain or vanilla)

½   banana (You can keep these fresh on hand by skinning them, breaking them in half and freezing in baggies)

1   cup frozen fruit (blueberries, strawberries, peaches)

3 or 4 ice cubes

       sugar to taste (this is up to you; you can add a teaspoon which will make this sweeter)

Blend all ingredients in blender. If you want your smoothie thicker or more frozen, you can use more ice. *2 servings.*

This is a healthy drink! It's great for breakfast, lunch or just a snack! My teenagers drink these all the time! They put anything they find in the refrigerator in them, orange juice, yogurt, whatever I have on hand! You can even mix your fruits together, to make this even more tasty! Frozen blueberries are especially great!

Calories 115
Protein .... 3.8 G
Carbohydrates .... 24 G
Dietary Fiber .... 2.7 G
Fat Total .... 1.5 G
Fat Saturated 0
Sodium .... 50 Mg
Calories from fats 12%

Strawberry Banana Frozen Fruit

1	6 ounce can pink lemonade
1	20 ounce can crushed pineapple
1	16 ounce box of frozen strawberries with juice
1	6 ounce jar maraschino cherries with juice (cut in half)
3	6 ounce cans of water
½	cup sugar (may use less)
4-5	sliced bananas

Mix all the ingredients in a large Jello mold, bundt pan, or glass casserole dish. Freeze for several hours. To serve, run warm water on bottom of jello mold or bundt pan, and cut into squares! This is pretty served on a bed of lettuce! *12 servings. Jill Seagrave- Springfield, Missouri.*

Kids love this! It's especially good on a hot day! These can be individually wrapped and placed in the freezer for quick snacks! This is a great summer dessert! You can cut this into individual pieces and wrap and freeze!

Calories 146
Protein .... 0.874 G
Carbohydrates .... 37.7 G
Dietary Fiber .... 2.35 G
Fat-Total .... 0.310 G
Fat-Saturated .... 0.084 G
Sodium .... 2.77 Mg
Calories from fats 2%

Frozen Banana Shake

2	sliced bananas
1	cup skim milk
1	cup frozen vanilla yogurt (fat-free)
1	cup ice cubes

Combine all ingredients and blend in blender until blended. This has a very frothy consistency. *2-4 servings. 8 ounces.*

You can add strawberries to these to make a fresh fruit drink. This makes a great breakfast drink, snack, or sweet dessert drink. Once your family discovers how many smoothies and shakes that they can make using fruit, your blender will never be clean! I know, since mine is always in the sink!

Calories 159
Protein .... 6.24 G
Carbohydrates .... 34.4 G
Dietary Fiber .... 1.53 G
Fat-Total .... 0.511 G
Fat-Saturated .... 0.236 G
Sodium .... 86.0 Mg
Calories from fats 3%

Mango Shake

4 or 5   mango spears (these come in a jar in the refrigerated section in the super market) you may also slice from fresh mangos

1   cup low-fat yogurt (you my use vanilla or flavor of your choice)

½   banana

¼   cup pineapple chunks

4 or 5   ice cubes

Blend all ingredients in your blender until smooth. This makes a tasty breakfast drink! *4 servings. ¾ cup.*

These shakes can be made with anything healthy you have in your refrigerate. Experiment!

Calories 106
Protein .... 2.2 G
Carbohydrates .... 22.9 G
Dietary Fiber .... .6 G
Fat Total .... .8 G
Fat Saturated .... 0 G
Sodium .... 29 Mg
Calories from fats .... .07%

Me Maws' Banana Bread

3	ripe or over ripe bananas
1	cup sugar
2	egg whites
1½	cups all purpose flour
2	tablespoons margarine
1	teaspoon baking soda
1	teaspoon salt

Mash bananas with a fork. Add rest of ingredients. Bake in a floured loaf pan at 325° for 60-80 minutes. Check with toothpick. Some ovens vary on rate of cooking. *8 servings or 1 loaf. Doris Stinnett- St. Louis, Missouri.*

This makes a wonderful loaf of banana bread. Great for breakfast or anytime!

Calories 256
Protein .... 3.77 G
Carbohydrates .... 52.9 G
Dietary Fiber .... 1.49 G
Fat-Total .... 3.80 G
Fat-Saturated .... 0.605 G
Sodium .... 449 Mg
Calories from fats 13%

Chewy Granola Cookies

1½	cups sifted, unbleached white flour
½	teaspoon baking powder
¾	teaspoon baking soda
½	teaspoon salt
2	eggs
1	teaspoon cinnamon
½	teaspoon ginger
¼	cup brown sugar
¼	cup granulated sugar
⅓	cup safflower oil
½	cup molasses
2	cup low-fat granola with raisins

Combine flour, baking powder, baking soda, salt, cinnamon, ginger, and sugar in a mixing bowl. Add oil, eggs, molasses, and granola. Mix until blended. Dough will be soft. Drop by teaspoon on a nonstick cookie sheet (can spray with Pam first). Bake at 350° for 7-8 minutes. Cool. Do not overbake. These are great, chewy. *Makes 24 medium cookies.*

These are an easy, healthy oatmeal raisin cookie! Make 2 batches and you can freeze these!

Calories 112
Protein .... 1.43 G
Carbohydrates .... 19.4 G
Dietary Fiber.................. 0.609 G
Fat-Total .... 3.45 G
Fat-Saturated .... 0.410 G
Sodium .... 96.0 Mg
Calories from fats 27%

Fresh Fruit Kabobs

1	quart strawberries (whole)
2	medium size ripe cantaloupe, cut into 1-1 ½ inch chunks
1	medium honey dew melon, cut into 1-1 ½ inch chunks (optional)
2	6 ounce containers Yoplait fat-free Yogurt(I use strawberry)
1	small container Cool Whip lite
1	4 ounce package wooden skewers

Arrange fruit on skewers, alternating melon and strawberries (the berries look pretty with the leaves left on). Mix yogurt and Cool Whip together. You may not need all of the Cool Whip. Add the amount you desire. Arrange skewers on a pretty plate with your dip served in the middle. *20 servings. 1 kabob lightly dipped.*

Variation on Dip:

1	package vanilla instant pudding made with skim milk
1	small container Cool Whip lite

Mix the 2 together. This makes a good fruit dip too!

This makes a pretty fruit platter for desserts or just as a snack appetizer!

Calories 111
Protein .... 1.63 G
Carbohydrates .... 20.4 G
Dietary Fiber .... 2.78 G
Fat-Total .... 2.56 G
Fat-Saturated .... 2.17 G
Sodium .... 19.6 Mg
Calories from fats. 21%

Fresh Peach Dumplings

5	large peaches peeled and sliced
1	cup sugar
2	cup water
5	tablespoons lemon juice
1	cup pancake mix
¼	cup packed brown sugar
¼	teaspoon ground nutmeg
½	cup skim milk
2	tablespoon vegetable oil (preferably Canola)

Vanilla frozen Yogurt (Edy's makes a fat-free)
Fresh mint to garnish (optional)

Combine first 4 ingredients, and bring to a boil. In a separate bowl, combine pancake mix, brown sugar, and nutmeg. Add oil and milk and stir until dry ingredients are moist. Drop by tablespoon into boiling peach mixture. Cover and reduce heat to low. Cook 15 minutes with the lid on. Remove and serve over frozen yogurt. Can add juice to as well. *8 servings. 2 dumplings + 1-2 scoops of yogurt.*

This is a different way to serve fresh peaches! I tried it on my neighbor Brad C. who has a sweet tooth, and he gave it an "A"!

Calories. 330
Protein .... 6.45 G
Carbohydrates .... 69.5 G
Dietary Fiber.................. 0.971 G
Fat-Total .... 4.27 G
Fat-Saturated .... 0.232 G
Sodium .... 306 Mg
Calories from fats............... 11%

Strawberry Angel

1	angel food cake
1	8 ounce cream cheese (Philadelphia brand "free")
¼	cup sugar
1	8 ounce Cool Whip lite or free Cool Whip
1	teaspoon vanilla
1	quart sliced strawberries
1	14 ounce package strawberry glaze (you may use sugar-free or regular)

Crumble cake in 9 x 13 pan. Mix sugar, cream cheese, vanilla, and Cool Whip together and spread over cake. Mix glaze with strawberries, pour on top of cream cheese layer and refrigerate. *10 servings. Jeanette Hutcheson- Springfield, Missouri.*

You can reduce the amount of sugar in this if you prefer. To serve, cut into squares. This won't be around long! Everyone loves this, so be prepared to give out the recipe!

Calories 181
Protein .... 4.10 G
Carbohydrates .... 30.8 G
Dietary Fiber .... 1.55 G
Fat-Total .... 3.06 G
Fat-Saturated .... 2.85 G
Sodium .... 192 Mg
Calories from fats 15%

Lemon Angel Food Cake

1   angel food cake
1   small package Instant lemon pudding
       (mix as directed using 2 cups skim milk)
1   small package lemon jello
       (mix with 1 cup boiling water)
1   small container Cool Whip (lite brand)

Tear cake into bite size pieces. Arrange in bundt cake pan. Mix pudding and jello together and let cool until it thickens a little. Pour evenly over cake. Spread Cool Whip over pudding mixture and refrigerate until firm. *8-10 servings. Kim Russell- Lebanon, Missouri.*

If you prefer making a home made angel food cake, there are many varieties available and remember they are all "fat-free." This is another recipe you will be asked for! This will be gone as soon as you start to serve it!

Calories 167
Protein .... 3.10 G
Carbohydrates .... 28.2 G
Dietary Fiber .... 0 G
Fat-Total .... 3.65 G
Fat-Saturated .... 3.62 G
Sodium .... 140 Mg
Calories from fats 21%

Healthy
Strawberry Banana
Parfait

1   small container strawberry fat-free yogurt
       (stir so fruit is evenly distributed)
1   sliced small banana
3-4   tablespoons low-fat granola with raisins
3-4   tablespoons lite Cool Whip

Spoon 2 tablespoons yogurt into bottom of parfait glass or
wine glass. Add slices of banana, top with 1 tablespoon
granola and a dab of Cool Whip. Repeat layers and sprinkle
yogurt with granola on top. End up with a dab of cool whip
on top. *1 serving.*

This makes a quick, easy, and pretty dessert you could even
serve to company or also a wonderful healthy breakfast! You
can use any fresh fruit or yogurt for this. This is a recipe that
you can have fun with and change any way you like! The
kids like it too!
If you were making this for company, you could look for the
larger carton of yogurt. Sometimes the supermarkets carry
some of the flavors in the larger sizes.

Calories 285
Protein .... 7.36 G
Carbohydrates .... 56.9 G
Dietary Fiber .... 3.01 G
Fat-Total .... 3.26 G
Fat-Saturated .... 2.45 G
Sodium .... 108 Mg
Calories from fats 10%

Brownies a la Mode

1   box of low-fat brownie mix baked and cut into 18-20 brownies
1   15 ounce container Hershey's fat-free chocolate syrup
1   quart fat-free frozen yogurt (vanilla)

Bake brownies according to package directions. Cool. Cut into squares. Top each brownie with 1-2 scoops of frozen yogurt. Drizzle with 1 tablespoon of warm syrup. I microwave the syrup to heat. *18 servings. 1 brownie and ½ cup ice cream.*

This is one of those simple desserts you will get raves about! There are many box brownie mixes out, and new brands come out all the time. So look carefully, and read your labels! Choose a lighter version such as Lovin' Lites. These will only have 1-2 grams of fat per cut brownie.

Calories 274
Protein .... 6.62 G
Carbohydrates .... 57.2 G
Dietary Fiber .... 0.469 G
Fat-Total .... 2.77 G
Fat-Saturated .... 0.604 G
Sodium .... 191 Mg
Calories from fats 9%

Low-Fat Carrot Cake

3-4	large carrots, shredded
1	medium zucchini, shredded
3	cups all-purpose flour
½	cup sugar
2	teaspoons cinnamon
2	teaspoons baking soda
1	teaspoon salt
1	teaspoon baking powder
½	teaspoon ginger
1	20 ounce can crushed pineapple in unsweetened juice
1	cup packed light brown sugar
1	8 ounce container frozen egg substitute (thawed)
⅔	cup vegetable oil
1	tablespoon vanilla
1	cup raisins (may use baking raisins)
¾	cup powdered sugar
2 ½	teaspoons reserved pineapple juice

Shred carrots to make 2 cups. Shred zucchini to make 1 cup; set both aside. Preheat oven to 350° F. Spray 10 inch bundt pan with PAM. In large bowl, mix flour, sugar, cinnamon, baking soda, baking powder, salt and ginger. Drain pineapple, reserve juice. In medium bowl, with wire whisk or fork, mix drained pineapple, brown sugar, egg substitute, and vanilla until smooth. Stir in pineapple mixture, shredded carrots, and zucchini and raisins into flour mixture, just until moistened. Pour batter into bundt pan and bake 55 minutes. Cool. Mix powdered sugar and preserved pineapple juice for glaze. When cake is cooled, drizzle glaze over and serve. *10-12 servings. Suzy Hamelink- Charlotte, North Carolina.*

This has a wonderful flavor, and it's so healthy! Just think of all the veggies you are getting!

Calories	304
Protein	4.50 G
Carbohydrates	71.8 G
Dietary Fiber	2.51 G
Fat-Total	0.496 G
Fat-Saturated	0.077 G
Sodium	430 Mg
Calories from fats	1%

Sinfully Healthy Index

Please send_____copies of **Sinfully Healthy**

@ $ 14.95 (U.S.) each $_____

Plus postage/handling @ $ 4.50 each $_____

Texas residents add sales tax @ $.90 each $_____

Check or Credit Card (Canada-credit card only)   Total $_____

Charge to my ❏ [MasterCard] or ❏ [VISA]

Account # _____

Expiration Date _____

Signature _____

> Mail, Fax or E-Mail:
> Debbi Stinnett
> 3237 A E. Sunshine
> PMB #107
> Springfield, MO 65804
> (417) 883-3868 Fax
> debsinfulhealthy@sbcglobal.net
> For more information,
> please e-mail Debbi Stinnett @
> debsinfulhealthy@sbcglobal.net

Name _____

Address _____

City _____ State _____ Zip _____

Phone (day) _____ (night) _____

— —

Please send_____copies of **Sinfully Healthy**

@ $ 14.95 (U.S.) each $_____

Plus postage/handling @ $ 4.50 each $_____

Texas residents add sales tax @ $.90 each $_____

Check or Credit Card (Canada-credit card only)   Total $_____

Charge to my ❏ [MasterCard] or ❏ [VISA]

Account # _____

Expiration Date _____

Signature _____

> Mail, Fax or E-Mail:
> Debbi Stinnett
> 3237 A E. Sunshine
> PMB #107
> Springfield, MO 65804
> (417) 883-3868 Fax
> debsinfulhealthy@sbcglobal.net
> For more information,
> please e-mail Debbi Stinnett @
> debsinfulhealthy@sbcglobal.net

Name _____

Address _____

City _____ State _____ Zip _____

Phone (day) _____ (night) _____